Cross-Train Your Brain

To my family, friends, and colleagues, who always believed I'd write this book.

Cross-Train Your Brain

A Mental Fitness Program for Maximizing Creativity and Achieving Success

Stephen D. Eiffert

American Management Association

New York • Atlanta • Boston • Chicago • Kansas City • San Francisco • Washington, D.C.
Brussels • Mexico City • Tokyo • Toronto

Library of Congress Cataloging-in-Publication Data

Eiffert, Stephen D.
    Cross-train your brain : a mental fitness program for maximizing
creativity and achieving success / Stephen D. Eiffert.
        p.   cm.
    Includes bibliographical references and index.
    ISBN 0-8144-7994-4 (pbk.)
    1. Creative ability.   2. Creative thinking.   I. Title.
BF408.E395   1999
153.4—dc21   98–17348
                                                          CIP

Printing number

10   9   8   7   6   5   4   3   2   1

Contents

Preface

There is an optimist hidden in each and every one of us. We work hard expecting to provide a better future, but few of us realize the potential that is inherent in us—the potential that does not depend on our work, our families, or our hobbies. That potential can be found in our brains.

Our brains are what distinguishes us from the animals, and they are also what distinguishes our "selves." Yet, our brains need training just like any other part of the body if they are to function at maximum capacity. "Sure," you may say. "I went to school. I have a master's degree, and I continue to keep abreast of current events—especially those that affect my job."

Although this is commendable, research has shown that there is more to brain development than just receiving information. In order to grow, one must train the brain to work in new ways. This idea is the heart of cross-training. We all have different interests and distinct patterns that we fall into in life. The theory of cross-training encourages us to look closely at where those interests and patterns lie and challenge them. If you love books, for example, set aside time to learn to work with your hands. If you are a musician, play a word game such as Scrabble. In short, train your brain by participating in activities that expand its power.

In the chapters that follow, I will walk you through a number of principles—truths about how our brains and our lives function. You cannot train your brain using a distinct method until you understand how it functions now. For each principle, I have included practical suggestions and exercises. These are not all-encompassing, however. You can expand your brain power in millions of little ways, but these exercises are designed to give you a practical head-start on cross-training.

I make the assumption that you are fairly well-entrenched in modern western culture. For example, most Americans today do not actually see themselves as creative. Developing creativity, then, has become a major thrust of this book. I address creativity, however, not in the most common sense applied to artists and musicians, but with the understanding that creativity plays a role in every part of our lives. Problem solving, business negotiations, inventions, and human relationships all require a bit of creativity to be handled most successfully. Ultimately, this book is designed to aid you in developing success in those aspects of your life that you most value.

Introduction

Get Ready, Get Set . . .

"One can never be content to creep when one feels an impulse to soar."

—Helen Keller

When our bodies are not properly attended to, we grow weak. We all recognize the value of training our bodies through a variety of exercises—muscle building, endurance building, and coordination enhancing. What many of us do not realize, however, is the need to train our minds in the same manner.

Our brains are an important part of our bodies. In fact, many of us would say it is the most important. The brain is what distinguishes human beings from other animals, and it is what makes us different from other human beings. The human brain is an adaptive mechanism of enormous sophistication; it's the most complex system currently known in the universe.

Traditionally, you might think of cross-training as becoming proficient in a related task or skill. This type of cross-training enables the individual to increase his or her performance in an area of specialty. But truly transformative changes have been shown to occur when individuals learn in areas that initially seem unrelated to existing skills.

The goal of cross-training is to awaken you to the enormous potential of your mind. We all start with the same raw materials—about three pounds of gray matter. But we all shape our brains differently through a lifetime of experiences. The tremendous range of adaptability afforded as a result of our sophisticated brain has enabled us to survive where other species have become extinct. Historically, however, biological adaptability has occurred at a slow and unconscious level—brought on by pressures exerted from environmental conditions. What many people do not realize, though, is that you can take an active role now in shaping your brain through activities and exercise. These exercises are designed to (1) make you aware of the way you think and (2) aid you in forming new thinking patterns where desired.

Cross-training is about both internal changes of awareness and external changes in actions. When you begin the practice of cross-training, you break your tasks into small steps to progress in the direction of your vision. Although the steps may be relatively simple, the overall task may require great effort. Real, meaningful change comes from the slow process of conscious, continuous practice over time.

Why Cross-Train?

Opening the mind to the possibility of solution-thinking (envisioning options) and releasing it from the recurring habit of problem-thinking (being held to conditions) is the benefit of cross-training. This new perspective can affect your life on a professional, personal, and spiritual level. Professionally, you can improve your productivity through new ideas and new solutions to old problems. Cross-training could also enable you to better understand and respond to office dynamics. You might even want to involve subordinates in some cross-training techniques to improve their performance. Personally, cross-training enables you to improve relationships at home through exercises such as perspective shifts. Spiritually, cross-training enables you to develop a new understanding of life and your role in the universe. This comprehension leads to achieving a greater sense of fulfillment in life.

Of course, cross-training is also fun. Those who exercise regularly will tell you they see a payoff in the form of a healthier body, but they also come to enjoy the process—the exercise itself. Cross-training your brain is no different. The ultimate payoff of cross-training can be seen in terms of products—ideas you would not have had otherwise and an ability to see and gain control over limitations. As a bonus, it is also an enjoyable process.

A Framework for Cross-Training

Three aspects to cross-training help you unlock your thinking and behavior to facilitate change: principle, process, and practice. These powerful concepts, working together, release the insights and actions necessary to redefine our thinking and redirect our actions, enabling us to begin working within our creative, formative minds.

Principle

Principles are the infrastructure of cross-training. Principles are the foundations of thought and action, which bring understanding to human events. Principles are conditions that exist even when you do not understand them or have no knowledge of their existence.

In the physical sciences, principles are often called laws. Many of the laws of matter correspond with the principles of mind. In physical science, we understand that force in one direction will be matched by an equal force in the other. A pendulum demonstrates this classic law. Push something far enough in one direction, and it will respond by overreacting in the opposite direction. This same principle applies to people. One of the fundamental principles of the eastern philosophy of Taoism is that when something reaches its extreme in one direction, it will revert to the other. Thus, nature encourages us to seek the middle way, the way of balance.

Principles underlie our thoughts and actions. Uncovering and understanding them is important, because they can explain and reveal your actions. Principles of cross-training might include the following phrases: "You create your own life expectancy," or, "Everyone is your teacher."

Principles, however, are not the same as truths. Like principles, truths always incorporate the lower into the higher. They seek to explain observations in general terms. But truth is context-based. Truth may vary depending on numerous conditions. Time is a condition that can affect truth, as in, "What is true today may not be true tomorrow." Perspective is also an arbitrator of truth. On the witness stand, individuals are sworn to tell the truth, the whole truth, and nothing but the truth. Time and time again, we observe two people with contradictory recall or perceptions of the same event. Is one of them lying? Or, are they each reporting the truth as they see it?

Truth can also be condition-based. You may believe that taking a life is a crime. Conversely, you may hold the belief that if a person is found guilty of killing another, it is not killing when society executes that individual. Truths are often anchored in a society's or individual's belief system or world view. Truths are important, but they are not the same as universal laws.

Principles are not events. They are revealed through patterns of events. Too often people spend too much time focused on the event, or condition level, of thinking. At the event thinking stage, you expend all your energy responding to a specific event and fail to see that a pattern of these types of events seems to be recurring over and over again. Television news coverage is, for the most part, event-focused. It reports daily on crime, government corruption, child abuse, and natural disasters, without ever attempting to get behind the event and look at the processes and patterns that seem to be at work. It is your responsibility to use your creative mind to observe patterns behind the events. Then, your insight into a broader context of understanding is enhanced. You get a bigger picture.

You can discover principles as they apply to your own life by applying your creative formative thinking to your everyday experiences. Principles will sometimes provide instant insight when they reveal themselves as a problem or when a situation arises. Other times, the insight will be delayed and will arrive only after the event. Seeking to understand principles and how they contribute to expan-ding your creative abilities is the practice of a fully functioning person. What's more, maximizing your creative nature requires the discovery of universal principles. Identifying a principle and its hidden power to control us usually comes through your observation of a process.

Process

Processes are the way things happen. They are the recurring patterns, or relationships of action and results, that when observed point the way to uncovering the principle. Processes are also the actions over which you ultimately have control and that you can consciously change.

The process of changing your mind to change your outcome is not difficult, but it does take time. Most people seem to go through three stages of awareness of processes and their own role in how their response creates their lives.

1. Blame. At this level of awareness, one is focused on the event or outcome. One may ask of a situation, "Why does this always happen to me?" This person has not yet identified the principle or process at work in some situation that is holding back creative thinking. Much blaming and accusing of others happens at this level.

2. Self-acknowledgment. This individual begins to see a pattern in situations and events. He is beginning to become process-focused. This individual has become aware of how he might need to hold himself responsible for this recurring pattern in thoughts and actions.

3. Self-responsibility. This individual chooses to focus on making a change using some new process. He sees consequences to particular actions and thoughts and chooses to consciously change behaviors. This results in a changed experience and often a changed outcome.

Intuitively, we all understand that stage three is the most productive stage. But discovering these patterns in your life and making a conscious effort to change them takes practice. For example, you may observe that losing your temper with subordinates when they make a mistake does not do much to improve your relationships and usually upsets your stomach. You can then consciously identify a new process to employ when subordinates make errors. You might ask them to replay the event, recounting what occurred and what they recommend to ensure that it does not occur again. If you discover after a few weeks of practicing this new process that individual performance seems to improve and your stomach has not been upset once, you have created a better experience and outcome by accessing a deeper level of understanding using your creative mind. You changed your process.

Attempting different processes in your efforts to improve conditions can result in deeper insights about principles. As you begin to notice patterns in behavior or activities, you can then look behind the patterns to discover what causal principles are at work. It may be that your relationship with your son parallels the process you observed in dealing with subordinates. Anger and blaming does not seem to be creating a better experience or outcome for you at home as well. Now you are working at the deep creative mind level, uncovering principles and processes that have been manipulating your behavior.

Habit and conditions may have caused these practices to form unconsciously and with no regard for your true desires. Changing them, however, must be a conscious practice fueled by your desire for a better outcome.

Practice

Practice is the force of change. It is only through the repetition of practicing a new behavior or thought process that we bring about the desired changes in our lives. Nothing consciously changes without the sustained commitment of practice. Of course, practice is not completely an uphill battle. As you begin to have success changing specific behaviors, you will find the rewards are significant enough to reinforce the practice.

In addition, success in one area may lead you to look closely for related principles that may also have bearing on your life. For example, the individual who began by changing his angry behavior may begin to invest more attention to the relationship of his body and his feelings. He may discover another related principle—garbage in, garbage out—and choose to improve his life through regular exercise and a healthy diet.

Putting It All Together

Principle, process, and practice are the combined forces of cross-training effectiveness. When you understand which principle or principles are at work, you are able to identify which processes you need to practice to change your experience and outcome.

Imagine that you are on a business team that meets monthly to discuss problems and opportunities for improving customer service. Your meetings always seem to follow a similar pattern. They are slow starting because the same people are frequently late. Once everyone arrives, too much time is spent chit-chatting. When the meeting is finally underway, a handful of people dominate the conversation while another group does not participate much. Arguments are frequent regarding opinions. One or two negative, outspoken individuals seem to regularly bring the group energy down. The meeting breaks up without most ideas being finalized or any action plans being made. Too many meetings are unfortunately just like this.

Allowing this process to continue will make it increasingly difficult to effect change, because the negative energy in the group will grow over time. Applying the principle, process, practice approach, we can identify opportunities for change. The underlying principle can be found in the processes observed. You observe that "negativity breeds negativity" and "expectations create inertia." By identifying these principles, you also reveal some potentially positive process changes.

You may choose to conduct an informal benchmarking study to help you identify positive meeting practices. You look for these practices in organizations that have successful meetings and adapt their ideas to your meeting situation.

You also discover that your team needs to establish some guidelines to clarify values, mutual respect, and acceptable and unacceptable behavior. Examples of these guidelines might include:

→ Critical thinking is invited; negative or derogatory remarks are discouraged.
→ Punctual attendance is required.
→ Attendees are expected to be prepared with written reports prior to every meeting.
→ Agendas need to be set with specific timeliness.
→ Minutes and assignments need to be kept in writing, and adhered to.
→ Team roles should be assigned, such as facilitator, timekeeper, scribe, rule observer, and so on.
→ A team thinking and problem-solving process should be learned and practiced at all sessions.
→ Meetings should be more fun.

Of course, identifying potentially successful processes is just the first step. Only through practicing them will improved experiences and outcomes become consistent. This practice may take time, but long term change cannot be quickly fixed.

The Transformative Power of Writing Practice

Writing is probably the best cross-training tool available in aiding us in the discovery of principles. It provides us an awareness of ourselves and our environment that few other exercises can. Simply through the process of daily writing one can uncover the negative processes that limit one's potential and begin revealing the process of self discovery of our unlimited potential. We discover the greatest changes when practice is sustained over time.

Over the years I have found many fellow travelers who praise the rewards of daily writing. Julie Cameron in *The Artist's Way* calls it "morning pages." Natalie Goldberg in *Writing Down the Bones* calls it "taking out the trash." Call it what you will, journal writing is a form of meeting with yourself daily to discover what is going on inside. You may think you know what is happening without the practice of writing. I did. But until you begin communicating with yourself on paper every day, you really don't know or understand as much as you could.

I first began journal writing while in the military. A teenager, traveling about the world for the first time, I simply wrote as a way to keep track of my experiences. For nearly 20 years, as I grew a family and business, I sat the practice aside. One evening, as I sat in the audience listening to Bernie Seigal speak, he mentioned journal writing as one of his five steps of self awareness. That night I went home and wrote. I've never stopped.

Over the years I have filled many notebooks with my thoughts and feelings. It was cheaper than psycho-therapy and equally rewarding. And it's free. Journal writing has taught me many things about myself. I wrote on days when I didn't feel like it and didn't on days when I did. I came to realize that my feelings about writing were not as important as that I write each day. It was my first insight into the difference between the value of processes and outcomes. No one judged the results of my writing, but the process of bringing my self awareness onto a page where I could see and experience it allowed me to easily see recurring patterns and issues I still had not chosen to address.

I encourage you to include journal writing as an integral part of your cross-training practice. I seldom know what I will say each day when I pick up the pen. Some days I talk about something that is disturbing in my life; often I will discover what it is all about in the writing. Sometimes I write poetry because it seems to need to be written. Occasionally I write short stories, essays, character sketches, or song lyrics.

Often the ideas that come from inside arrive on the page without our awareness of where they came from or how they arrived. The process has created a channel or circuit that allows the creative energy to flow out of our otherwise inaccessible formative reservoir of unlimited potential. It gives voice and understanding to feelings, intuition, insight, and tremendous levels of self wisdom.

Over time you will begin to develop a relationship with your writing. You will find a voice to express thoughts and feelings that before had no way to be voiced. You may find this voice bleeding into your day-to-day life as well. You will discover things about yourself you didn't know. Some of it will please you, and some will make you sad. But you will always be glad for the discovery. You will begin to develop a relationship with your imagination that you would have never known possible. You will find that your ideas improve and your comfort with the creative process grows.

When all is said and done the importance of writing is in the process, not the outcomes. You may choose to read what you've written or not. Occasionally, I will go back through old journals and see what's been happening with me. Sometimes I'm surprised to see how far I've come. Other times I am surprised to see how little I've progressed. Or, you may wish to throw away your daily writings. Since the process of awakening your creativity through this daily practice is the primary concern, feel free to trash the product. It does not matter. The good has come out of the doing.

Do not begin writing with the expectation of becoming a writer. Expectation can take all the joy out of the simple practice. Write to become a discoverer, an explorer of the vast inner space of yourself, the sole adventurer into the final frontier where only you can go; write to seek and find what you are all about and what talents are buried under the personality you show the rest of the world.

Getting Started

Here are some simple suggestions:

1. Write truthfully. It can be boring or funny. You are not pleasing anyone. Express your feelings as openly as you can. Here on the page you can say those things you might not feel comfortable saying out loud. Leave nothing unsaid. If you occasionally find yourself stuck try clustering (discussed in Chapter 5). This circling technique, writing down key words and arranging them as they seem to order themselves most sensibly to your creative mind, is an excellent way to break writer's block. Another technique is to ask yourself a random question regarding some issue that is puzzling or concerning you, then write your response. To get you started, I've included topics you may wish to address in your journal at the end of each chapter in this book, but don't feel you need to stick to these.

2. Write quickly. Don't think about what you are going to say, just begin saying it before the thinking can begin.

3. Write longhand. With daily writing practice we are attempting to get deeper within ourselves. It has been my experience that writing longhand, on paper, is much more effective in this self-discovery process. Many people who do daily writing practice agree. The more primitive tactile experience of writing by hand seems to get more heartfelt creative results. Try it and see.

4. Set aside a time. Although you may choose to write at any time, do it the same time each day. Mornings and evenings seem to be the best time for most people. Spend at least 15 minutes each day with your writing. You may get 2 pages or 3. Some days, if you are on a roll, keep it up as long as you like.

5. Minimize distractions. Find a quiet place and put aside all the other things and thoughts that might distract you from the writing. Find different places to write. When the weather is nice write outside in the morning or evening. On weekends take your notebook on your walk or drive.

6. Choose your tools. The notebook should be aesthetically appealing and easy to carry with you when you travel. Keep it in a private place if you are concerned about others finding your writing. It can be difficult to put your deepest most revealing thoughts on the page if you fear someone else might read them and not understand. The pen should be kind to your hands. You may want to choose one that writes in your favorite color. In the early stages of developing a new practice little things that make this ritual special will be helpful.

7. Try writing with the other hand. For a real change of pace write down your answers with your non-dominant hand. If you are right handed, use you left hand for journaling practice once in a while. Aside from the messy handwriting, you might be surprised what comes out of your mind.

8. Share with others. If you have a friend who also does daily writing, do it together sometimes. If it's comfortable, share what you've written. It can be a most delightful discovery to find that others have the same deep feelings and senses about the world that you have. We are all seeking our creative voice.

Conclusion

The journey to greater creative functionality is never ending. Stimulating yourself to operate in a more enlightened and higher performance manner will require a little knowledge about how your system currently works and about the principles of how things work. It will also require a commitment to making a few changes and surrendering some of the old processes that aren't working for you anymore. It will require you to experiment with new processes and observe the results. Finally, it will also require a commitment to practice. If you enjoy the adventure of discovery, however, there is no more interesting place to begin discovering than yourself.

At the end of each chapter you will find questions, exercises, and activities for you to ponder and work through as you read this book. Many of the individual exercises are designed to stimulate the self-questioning practice common to creative questers. Take time to think and work through each item, you may wish repeat exercises to see how the experiences change as you progress. Observe your results and feelings without judgment or comparison to others. Enjoy the process and delight in the journey of awakening your creative mind.

Journal Practice

Uncovering Processes in Your Behavior.

1. Observe your behavior regarding things you don't enjoy doing yet persist in doing in spite of your displeasure.

2. Make a list of the behaviors you have that cause you discomfort or displeasure. Keep a record of the amount of time you spend with them, how you feel before and after you do them.

3. When you discover a behavior you feel undermines your creative expression, look for patterns that may have occurred in the past. What principles do you think are behind these behaviors? Start a list.

4. Do you feel strongly enough about these activities that you would like to change them? What practices might you institute to begin making changes in these areas? How often are you willing to practice? When are you going to start?

Thanks to Ben Rook for the upside-down illustration and Bruce Helm for his graphics layout for the tests and quizzes.

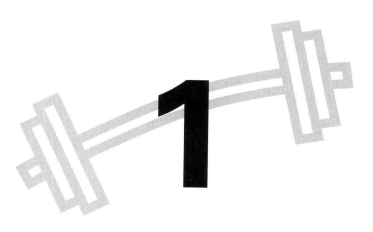

We are all born creative but lose our creative drive over our lifetimes.

"In the beginner's mind there are many possibilities, but in the expert's there are few."
—Shunryu Suzuki

Principle

For many years, creative thinking processes were believed to be reserved for the select few. In recent years, that idea has been debunked with the realization that everyone shares the same mental construct. With the exception of injury or mental dysfunction, which represents 10 to 15 percent of the population, all of us have the same ability to engage in the creative experience. As a child, you arrived in this world with an unlimited potential for creating. With each passing day, you give away more and more of that creative potential. A child loses up to 75

1

percent of his or her creativity between the ages of five
and seven. By the time adults are 40, most are expressing
less than two percent of the measurable creativity they
demonstrated as young children. Thus, the ability must be
reawakened and trained with encouragement and practice uncommon to most of us.

Creativity is not a trait. Unlike the color of your
eyes, whether you are left-handed or right-handed, or
tall or short, creativity is not a quality that is inherently
lesser or greater in some people. Your creative ability is
an aspect of your essential nature. Creativity is an attitude of expectation that realizes itself. Your expectation
of creativity fosters its own growth and expression. The
more you expect, the more you manifest in your life. This
reinforces you to expect even more.

Definition of Creativity

Author and consultant Edward de Bono incorporates
three diverse concepts into his definition of creativity.
First, he writes that "at the simplest level *creative* means
bringing into being something that was not there before."
He later adds, "The new thing must have value," and
finally, it must include the concepts of "unexpectedness
and change."[1]. Although this is an excellent definition, it
does little to express the common perception of the word
creativity. Most of us understand creativity in terms of
specific activities or feelings.

I asked a friend's 4-year-old grandson what creativity meant, and without hesitation he responded, "Doing
something fun."

Once I challenged my college class to help me
define the word creativity. Reading them the standard
Webster's definition, I recognized among several students
that slightly tight-eyed look that says, "I'm not sure that

---

[1] Edward de Bono, *Serious Creativity* (New York: Harper Business, 1992),
page 3.

definition does it for me." Responses were slow in coming. In an effort to stimulate them I asked, "What, then, do you think the opposite of creativity is?" Suddenly the answers began to flow, and I found them to be as diverse as they were surprising. Boring, routine, outdated, blind, unoriginal, unhappy, and so on were some of the responses. I began to see a pattern developing. Each student was defining how the lack of creativity would affect their lives. Their descriptions of the absence of creativity depicted bleak and unhappy conditions.

Some students defined creativity with regard to a specific act, like the 4-year-old who understood it when doing it. Playing music, drawing, and working on a project were examples they offered in their attempt to define the word. I began to see that we understand creativity most when we are either experiencing it or when we feel we have lost it. Creativity is a word that resists the confines of simple definition and it is a concept much broader than any specific application.

Creativity and creative are words people can use to express how they live, how they communicate ideas, how they do their jobs, and how they deal with relationships. Creativity is a process that expands your choices and releases your potential into some form of expression. In this book I will explore creativity as it applies to expanding your awareness of your potential—however that might manifest itself.

Value of Creativity

When you are acting from your creative nature, you are not necessarily doing something that no one else has ever done before; you are doing something you may have never done before, or you are doing something in a way you've never done it before. The act of creativity is exploring new ways to think, be, and express yourself. Creativity is a way of expanding yourself and celebrating your uniqueness in the universe. Creative action need not even be immediately useful, other than its role in changing the perspective of the creator. Often creative action leads to nothing other than a new insight or the liberation of new thoughts or attitudes.

Becoming more creative involves stepping outside the box that says your actions and activities must always be measured by the constraints of external value, time, or approval. Listening more to yourself, you will find your own barometer for valuing your creative actions. It all begins when you become what psychologist Carl Rogers once called "the fully functioning person." That your actions have value to others is merely a pleasant by-product.

Ultimately, creativity should add value to your life. There should be a noticeable improvement in process or outcome. Creativity may lead to improved business decisions (an outcome) or simply more job satisfaction due to new ways of thinking about the business world. Creativity allows for the expression of your greatest possible self on a daily basis—whether your time is spent at work or at play.

Process

Creativity, then, is found in every human being. Unfortunately, many do not recognize the simple principle that fuels it. The first step to becoming more creative is to believe in your own creative potential.

Research compiled from all the studies (and there have been hundreds) shows that the one variable that most influences a person's creative expression and potential is their expectation. Nothing—education, birth order, country of origin, brain dominance, profession, even genetics—influences our creative potential more than expectation. Who we are, how long we live, and the quality of our experience is in a powerful way governed by our expectation. Creative people expect themselves to be more creative—to come up with a clever solution, to create better lives. They act on their positive expectations as if they were real. As a result, increased creativity becomes their reality. People get what they expect.

Simply choosing to emphasize the possible and positive over the negative is the first step in successfully cross-training yourself. The self talk that goes on inside your head must begin to shift from "I can't" and "I'll never," to "I will" and "I can." Becoming aware of your limiting language and replacing it with positive expectations for creative solutions starts the process of moving awareness into action. Since your actions are extensions of your attitudes and beliefs, a vital step of cross-training is gaining awareness of the thinking that is sabotaging your creative expression.

Once you shift your awareness, then you can change your attitude. Cross-training your attitude requires you to put your positive thinking into action. Whether addressing a broken faucet in the home or speaking out with an idea in a business meeting, taking positive action on your ideas launches you toward better outcomes. Initiating this effort, while difficult, often creates the energy that propels you forward to even higher levels of attainment.

What Makes Someone Creative

To reawaken your creativity, you must take conscious steps toward a creative mindset. Much of this can be accomplished by mimicking the characteristics of creative individuals.

Carl Rogers, an American psychologist of the Gestalt tradition, studied the way we grow and learn with emphasis on developing the potential of the human brain. In his book *On Becoming a Person*, he develops a classic theory of individual creativity. Rogers' theory includes three internal and two external conditions for individual creativity to flourish.

Inner conditions

1. Openness to experience. Essentially, the more open an individual is to all aspects of his experience the more alive he is to possibilities that exist. The first sets of limitations that must be addressed are imposed by ourselves. Rigid, inflexible, or defensive attitudes can undermine the individual's creative experience. One must surrender fears, anxieties, and the need for control in order to step into the creative unknown. This step can be difficult and requires what might be termed a leap of faith.

The operating system of a computer is constantly calculating and managing software in the background while the computer is on. Yet, most of us do not know, nor do we care to know, what it is really doing. Sometimes people's thinking operates at this same unconscious automatic level. People often act or react almost without thinking. When this occurs, they are no longer consciously choosing their thoughts, experiences, and feelings about events. They have lost control.

One of the first steps in cross-training is to become consciously aware of these unconscious processes, gaining greater control and a much more complete experience. This idea is counter-intuitive for most of us. Human brains prefer to choose specific patterns and repeat them. The brain favors repetition, so it can automate the activity to an unconscious operational level. Although a certain amount of automation is important to function efficiently (can you imagine having to think as hard about how to get a spoon to your mouth as a one-year-old does?), automation of thought processes can also cause you to lose the details of the moment. Routine behavior can make you mindless— driving to work without noticing the day, walking outside without smelling the flowers, or listening to someone without really hearing them.

One way of opening up to new experiences is to consciously choose to experience something unknown or unfamiliar. Perhaps you have heard of football coaches putting players in ballet classes, *National Basketball Association* (NBA) teams learning meditation, managers going on wilderness adventures, or organizations rotating their key managers to get a bigger picture of the nature of the business. In these examples, the benefits are not only valuable but can be profoundly life-changing. Challenges associated with thinking and doing in areas where no previous experiences or assumptions exist cause the participants to think about what they are doing in new and different ways. Each individual must choose how he or she can expand personal experiences. For me, it can be as simple as varying my route to work in the morning to stimulate a new awareness of experience, or as fear inducing as a first skydiving trip.

Through cross-training you shift your perspectives, which increases your possibilities and provides insight and awareness that stimulate higher levels of performance. This type of cross-training broadens understanding and awakens perceptions that can dramatically improve ability and performance.

2. An internal locus of evaluation. Gaining approval from others is not as important to the creative act as is internal validation. Your ability to rely upon your own judgment, even when it is based solely upon intuition or feelings, is important to the survival of a new or original idea. Learn to feel those feelings and sense that intuition becomes more important to you. Creative acts frequently meet with resistance from others when they are initially introduced. Their survival prior to external validation usually depends upon a strong advocate: you.

3. The ability to toy with elements or concepts. Playing is often devalued in our society and is considered the action of children. Emphasis on productive work makes many of us uncomfortable with the act of playing, piddling, messing around, or toying with things or ideas. Yet it is out of this process that new patterns emerge, giving rise to insights and possibilities. It is during this playing stage, people most often stumble on a great insight or "ah-ha" moment. Creativity is stimulated by play.

External conditions (those environments in which you feel comfortable creating)

1. Psychological safety. (You're OK being you.) Rogers presents three aspects that define this condition. First, you must accept that the individual has unconditional worth. This idea enables you to feel safe in expressing yourself in any manner to discover your broad range of possibilities. The first aspect comes hand-in-hand with the second—nonjudgment. Freedom of judgment from yourself and others enables you to have your own feeling about the creation. This freedom does not mean that another cannot have an opinion or even offer constructive criticism; rather, it eliminates one's creative expression from the external polarizing judgment of good and bad. The final element of psychological safety is empathy. This condition implies that the creator is not only accepted but also is understood without judgment.

Highly creative individuals have learned to accept that mistakes are a part of the creative process. Often what is learned by making a mistake enables a person to move closer to a solution. Creative people do not confuse their personal value with the learning process of trial and error. Mistakes are not bad or good. Failure does not make you a lesser person. Often, it is quite the opposite.

The history of creative discovery is built upon the backs of trial and error. Columbus mistook America for the East Indies; R.W. Macy went bankrupt seven times before his department store succeeded; and Mark McGwire only got hits once out of every three times at bat!

2. Psychological freedom. This idea is the final aspect of creative empowerment. By having creative freedom we are allowed to develop self-responsibility. Being free from imposed attitudes and desires is not unlike allowing a child to become an adult. This freedom in a healthy child enables him to discover where his own self-responsibilities lie.[2]

Being creative is not simply something you learn to do; rather, it is a way you learn to be, a way we once knew but have lost along the way. As you work to

---

[2] Carl R. Rogers, *On Becoming a Person* (Boston: Houghton Mifflin Company, 1961).

become more creative, you begin to uncover limiting assumptions that constrict your expression. Learning to identify these limiting assumptions, many of which operate at an unconscious level, and challenging your thinking about them, is the most critical step in learning to express your higher abilities.

You must continue to learn and practice the attitudes and skills that keep your natural creative processes alive and vital, or you will quickly lose your fluency. When you discontinue exercising your creativity, you begin to narrow your expression. The resulting inflexibility results in a sense of powerlessness that robs you of the joy of a more fulfilling life. Besides, it's not very fun.

Practice Exercise

How Creative Are You?

By Eugene Raudsepp

How creative are you? The following test helps you determine whether you have the personality traits, attitudes, values, motivations, and interests that make up creativity. This test is based on several years' study of attributes possessed by men and women in a variety of fields and occupations who think and act creatively.

For each statement write the appropriate letter: A=Agree; B=In between or don't know; C=Disagree.

Be as frank as possible. Try not to second-guess how a creative person might respond.

_____ 1. I always work with a great deal of certainty that I am following the correct procedure for solving a particular problem.

_____ 2. It would be a waste of time for me to ask questions if I had no hope of obtaining answers.

___ 3. I concentrate harder on whatever interests me than do most people.

___ 4. I feel that a logical step-by-step method is best for solving problems.

___ 5. In groups, I occasionally voice opinions that seem to turn some people off.

___ 6. I spend a great deal of time thinking about what others think of me.

___ 7. It is more important for me to do what I believe to be right than to try to win the approval of others.

___ 8. People who seem uncertain about things lose my respect.

___ 9. More than other people, I need to have things interesting and exciting.

___ 10. I know how to keep my inner impulses in check.

___ 11. I am able to stick with difficult problems over extended periods of time.

___ 12. On occasion, I get overly enthusiastic.

___ 13. I often get my best ideas when I am doing nothing in particular.

___ 14. I rely on intuitive hunches and feelings of "rightness" or "wrongness" when moving toward the solution of a problem.

___ 15. When problem solving, I work faster when analyzing the problem and slower when synthesizing the information I have gathered.

___ 16. I sometimes get a kick out of breaking the rules and doing things I am not supposed to do.

___ 17. I like hobbies that involve collecting things.

___ 18. Daydreaming has provided the impetus for many of my more important projects.

___ 19. I like people who are objective and rational.

___ 20. If I had to choose from two occupations other than the one I now have, I would rather be a physician than an explorer.

____ 21. I can get along more easily with people if they belong to about the same social and business class as myself.

____ 22. I have a high degree of aesthetic sensitivity.

____ 23. I am driven to achieve high status and power in life.

____ 24. I like people who are most sure of their conclusions.

____ 25. Inspiration has nothing to do with the successful solution of problems.

____ 26. When I am in an argument, my greatest pleasure would be for the person who disagrees with me to become a friend, even at the price of sacrificing my point of view.

____ 27. I am much more interested in coming up with new ideas than in trying to sell them to others.

____ 28. I would enjoy spending an entire day alone, just "chewing the mental cud."

____ 29. I tend to avoid situations in which I might feel inferior.

____ 30. In evaluating information, the source is more important to me than the content.

____ 31. I resent things being uncertain and unpredictable.

____ 32. I like people who follow the rule, "business before pleasure."

____ 33. Self-respect is much more important than the respect of others.

____ 34. I feel that people who strive for perfection are unwise.

____ 35. I prefer to work with others in a team effort rather than solo.

____ 36. I like work in which I must influence others.

____ 37. Many problems that I encounter in life cannot be resolved in terms of right or wrong solutions.

___ 38. It is important for me to have a place for everything and everthing in its place.

___ 39. Writers who use strange and unusual words merely want to show off.

___ 40. Following is a list of terms that describe people. Choose 10 words that best characterize you.

energetic	persuasive	observant
fashionable	self-confident	perservering
original	cautious	habit-bound
resourceful	egotistical	independent
stern	predictable	formal
informal	dedicated	forward-looking
factual	open-minded	tactful
inhibited	enthusiastic	innovative
poised	acquisitive	practical
alert	curious	organized
unemotional	clear-thinking	understanding
dynamic	self-demanding	polished
courageous	efficient	helpful
perceptive	quick	good-natured
thorough	impulsive	determined
realistic	modest	involved
absent-minded	flexible	sociable
well-liked	restless	retiring

How do you rate? See the following scoring method.

Scoring

To compute your score, circle and add up the values assigned to each item. The values are as follows:

	A Agree	B In-between or don't know	C Disagree
1.	0	1	2
2.	0	1	2
3.	4	1	0
4.	–2	0	3
5.	2	1	0
6.	–1	0	3
7.	3	0	3
8.	0	1	2
9.	3	0	–1
10.	1	0	3
11.	4	1	0
12.	3	0	–1
13.	2	1	0
14.	4	0	–2
15.	–1	0	2
16.	2	1	0
17.	0	1	2
18.	3	0	–1
19.	0	1	2
20.	0	1	2
21.	0	1	2
22.	3	0	–1
23.	0	1	2
24.	–1	0	2
25.	0	1	3
26.	–1	0	2
27.	2	1	0
28.	2	0	–1
29.	0	1	2
30.	–2	0	3

31.	0	1	2
32.	0	1	2
33.	3	0	2
34.	−1	0	2
35.	0	1	2
36.	1	2	3
37.	2	1	0
38.	0	1	2
39.	−1	0	2

40. The following have values of 2:

energetic	persevering	perceptive
original	independent	curious
resourceful	innovative	self-demanding
dedicated	dynamic	flexible
enthusiastic	courageous	involved
observant		

The following have values of 1:

informal	forward-looking	restless
self-confident	alert	determined
open-minded	thorough	

The rest have values of 0.

95–116	Exceptionally Creative
65–94	Very Creative
40–64	Above Average
20–39	Average
10–19	Below Average
Below 10	Noncreative

2

We all suffer from environmental limitations placed on our creativity.

"Human thought has its source in the divine fountain, which must be permitted to flow freely through man. Anyone who flows as life flows has solved the enigma of human existence and needs no other power. Anything evil blocks the flow of creative action."
—Lao Tzu

Principle

Our modern western world trains us to value logic and reasoning above intuition and emotion. Author William Manchester, in his book *A World Lit Only By Fire*, speculates that we began increased use of the left hemisphere of our brains during the latter part of the Middle Ages and early into the Renaissance era. Your brain consists

15

of two hemispheres—right and left. The right hemisphere houses our emotions and nonverbal thought processes. The left hemisphere houses our higher reasoning abilities and logical mind. It is also home to our ego—our sense of a separate self. (See Chapter 5, which discusses approaching life with our whole brain, for a more detailed discussion of the hemispheres.) Although the left hemisphere structure existed for thousands of years prior, it is speculated that before the 1500s, most daily functioning of the common man was located in the right hemisphere. As the left hemisphere became more used, the right hemisphere became underused.

The Modern Western World View

Numerous factors may have contributed to this change in world view that gradually took place through the Renaissance and Enlightenment periods. An increased exploration in arts and sciences went hand-in-hand with an increased ability and desire to explore the world.

Two major factors may have contributed to the developing emphasis of our left hemisphere. Mass publishing, as a result of the printing press, began to create accessible books in common languages. Reading became more widespread. Books provided the accessibility to abstract language and thought, which expanded our knowledge of a world outside the one in which we lived. This reading and abstract thinking process led to the development of a new sense of self as separate of others, extending man both physically and mentally.

The second factor was the development of a heightened awareness of time. The invention of clockwork allowed for a significant increase in precision over previous time-telling methods. The clock and its representation of time as an abstract or objective process caused the mind to acquire a sense of self outside the present moment and place. The Crusades, pilgrimages, and increased travel from the community of one's birth certainly also played a role in our mental development

Science and art, as well as the social pressures of new ideas about government, created a fertile mental environment where rapid mental growth occurred. The Age of Enlightenment and the belief that all was knowable reflected not only man's mental sophistication but also his arrogance.

There has been another, more recent change that affects creativity—the fact that our society, indirectly, no longer demands it. Before World War II, creativity was demonstrated through problem solving, discovery, invention, and the spontaneous expression of one's individual resourcefulness. If something was needed, you simply made it, fabricated it, or adapted it from something else. Without realizing it, much of the details of day-to-day living provided opportunities for creative problem solving and ingenuity. Evenings found people using their creativity to entertain themselves through music, storytelling, or crafts such as whittling and needlepoint.

The world changed quickly after World War II. With today's consumer marketing, an increasingly expanding variety of products makes creativity less necessary in our daily lives. Rather than being challenged to adapt products to specific situations, we are encouraged to buy new ones. In a society that finds itself with more dispensable income than dispensable time, we'd rather acquire than adapt.

The popularity of television and radio replaced the habit of entertaining ourselves. It became easier to buy art or music than learn to create it. We are actually discouraged from creative problem solving in the home.

Of course, the workplace presents an interesting dichotomy. The industrial revolution took creativity out of many jobs. The migration to the cities resulted in work found in repetitive and narrowly defined jobs. Frederick W. Taylor and Frank and Lillian Gilbreth conducted time and motion studies around the turn of the century, which precisely defined how a factory worker should move his body to maintain maximum efficiency. More recently, however, we are beginning to acknowledge that those corporations who recognize and encourage the creativity of their employees in the workplace have a jump on the competition. Total quality management gave the power back to the employee to stop the production line if a problem was spotted. Cellular manufacturing brings the factory closer to the tradesman, giving a team end-to-end responsibility for a product. Unfortunately, many employees have forgotten their natural creativity through a lifetime of limitations.

How We Learned Not to Be Creative

The brain is designed for learning. Each time a new piece of information is learned by the brain, the brain updates any areas where that new information can be used. This constant, readaptive process is what Cambridge University scholar and creativity guru Edward de Bono calls a self-organizing system. This self-organizing system is a complex system that contains all the resources for its own development, adaptation, change—even destruction. A self-organizing system adapts itself to the world, and at the same time it creates the world to which it is adapting. This co-creational relationship of external world to internal world has been in place for hundreds of millions of years.

Through the self-organizing process, the brain enables you to only recognize and see those patterns to which you have been previously exposed. Were the brain not involved in this filtering process, your awareness would be exposed to unlimited possible patterns, and you would be overwhelmed with the choices. Previously crafted neural pathways in your brain determine the patterns you will recognize. Those patterns have developed over time to adapt and match you to the environment in which you exist. You cannot hear like your dog or see like an eagle because your existence does not depend upon those particular abilities for survival.

Observe a five-year-old learning to tie his or her shoe. Intensely focusing and adjusting body language to get the working conditions correct, the child's little hands struggle as the face reflects the thought process being reviewed as the fingers work the laces. It can be painfully slow and often frustrating to observe this learning. Over a short period of time, the brain habitualizes—or conditions through habit—this routine until it can be done effortlessly. Once the pattern has been learned and the natural pathway created, it is not the nature of the brain to ask of itself, "Gee, I wonder if there is a better way to tie my shoes?"

The brain, now under control of the mind's programming, has self-organized itself around the pattern developed. It will not naturally seek out new patterns unless forced to do so. The mind will organize itself toward rote and repetition. Without this tendency, it could take us all day to put on our clothes. Every lesson would have to be relearned every time we encountered it. Without mental habits, there would be no time for anything else other than navigating the events of our daily activity.

This survival feature that nature has favored in the natural selection of the species is an example of unconscious thinking. Seeking patterns it already recognizes, the mind selectively chooses information that reinforces what it already believes it perceives in situations. Information that does not fit the pattern is filtered out.

Those things that we learn and repeat we self-organize ourselves to do habitually—without regard to good or bad, useful or wasteful. Left in its own unconscious mode, the mind chooses its habits indifferent of the availability of new methods or improvements which might actually provide superior functionality.

This self-organizing process of the brain, or pattern-making, determines the patterns we will see—*not* the patterns that exist. Events can be seen and interpreted in numerous ways, but nature and nurture favor predictability. This process of shaping and enculturation creates a knowledge base and belief system that mirrors the society in which it was created.

For hundreds of thousands of years, this simple and efficient system has worked. Thoughts, actions, and processes that increased survival became the thinking we have inherited and use today. Those patterns selectively evolved into our modern state without regard to their usefulness in the event of change. Your existing self-organized identity resists change. Conflict rises. You feel uncomfortable, anxious, or stressed when attempting to change. When this situation occurs and your struggle reveals limitations, you expect your mind to exercise creativity and provide you with solutions. Unfortunately, your self-organizing system has not prepared you to be creative. Self-organization has conditioned your mind to recognize familiar patterns, not create new ones.

Unchallenged, conditioning behaviors learned as a child profoundly affect how you act and react for the rest of your life, with regard to your range of expressions. Without consciously challenging existing patterns and creating new ones, you unconsciously harden your routines and become less flexible to change. Because many of your thinking patterns will become outdated over time, learning new ones is important for coping with change and maintaining a fulfilling life. The faster the external change occurs, the more quickly your thinking becomes outdated.

When exposed to new patterns the brain does not immediately recognize, it will attempt to conform information to known patterns to increase the likelihood of recognition or understanding. These underlying root metaphors, conceptual frameworks upon which information, thoughts, and understanding are conformed, are the paradigms upon which we force all new information. When a new pattern is formed or an old pattern is reformed in a new way, it creates a paradigm shift. A paradigm shift occurs when we get a new set of rules for playing an old game. This new set of rules causes us to rethink how we were previously playing the game and how we might play it in the future.

The Child's Mind

Once you were an artist. Once you were an explorer, a poet, a musician, an actor, and an athlete. Once you were everything you could imagine. Once you were a child. As a two-year-old, you did not have many mental patterns or expectations. You had not yet wired your brain to see the world, so everything you encountered was new—presenting you with unlimited learning possibilities. You were unlimited potential and boundless energy seeking direction.

How your mind develops is a product of the environment in which you were raised. Conscious and unconscious motivators shape its development. Your brain creates your mind with every experience and lesson you learn. You inherit the bundle of fears, inhibitions, attitudes, and prejudices upon which your society has collectively agreed. You learn the information your society acknowledges and ignore the information it eschews. You observe what you have been trained to observe and overlook what you have never been trained to see. No two minds, no matter how similar their influencing environment, are ever exactly the same—because no two individuals ever have exactly the same experiences. Even Chang and Eng Bunker, Siamese twins who lived their entire 63 years attached to one another, had different temperaments and mental abilities.

Your family, your peers, and your society have provided the conditioning experiences of your life. Each society has, when compared to another, vast differences in its thinking, communication, and understanding of the world. Eskimos have, for example, more than 70 different references for snow. The Mayan language had none. Aboriginal peoples still exist in a nonlinear time frame that manifests phenomena inexplicable by modern science. Songlines measure distances; mystical visions provide tribal leaders with guidance; and rain can be predicted long before logic can explain. A five-year-old Aboriginal child, a five-year-old Eskimo child, and a five-year-old from Columbus, Ohio, are already vastly different individuals in how they see the world, themselves, and their relationship to it.

At the time when your mental growth was occurring at its most accelerated rate, society and family made its greatest impact. As your natural curiosity developed along with your sense of self, your parents increased their direction and controlling actions. What is the first word your mom and dad taught you? No.

'No' and 'don't' are two words that stop the creative process. Two-year-olds hear these words from morning to night. Establishing acceptable and unacceptable behavior patterns is a way of culturally keeping children within the lines, clarifying safe and unsafe areas for us to explore, setting forth the foundational rules by which our tribe lives. On one hand, this activity is necessary to protect children from injuring themselves. On the other hand, it begins the process of making creative choices feel uncomfortable.

Parental directions serve to help the child fit into the culture of its birth so that it may adjust to the group and share the group's values and behaviors. Educational training creates the thinking that is representative of your future profession. As these patterns are created, the possibility of alternative patterns are ignored and slowly fade. It is not that you cannot have them, you just have not been wired to notice them. A child raised in the city recognizes far more of the city's environmental patterns than would a child raised in the country, and vice-versa.

Each aspect of a culture's communication is significant in this process. Tactile communication—touching, petting, holding—all send signals to the brain concerning what is being communicated and what is meant by that communication; which forms of tactile communication are acceptable and which are not. With whom, when, and where they may occur are also part of the instruction. Facial expressions and body language follow the same process.

By the age of five, much of the imprinting and organizing process has been established. Through conditioning, rewards, and punishment, people learn how to think and be a part of the tribe. Virginia Satir, a pioneer in family therapy, referred to these types of shaping behaviors as peoplemaking.

Because so much of this organizing behavior happens at an early age, the motivations behind and awareness of your thoughts and actions disappear as you fall into a cultural hypnosis—hypnosis in that we begin to feel, think, and act without conscious awareness. Thinking and behaving in the "right" way feels normal to you because it is the habit you have developed. Identity states such as class consciousness are formed. In societies with clear class consciousness, children learn early on in which class they belong and exhibit behavior that reinforces and affirms that mental position. Automatic gestures, postures, and even facial expressions are all in place.

At an early age, a wide range of behavioral responses to different roles are developing as your multiple selves: Who are you as the oldest child? Who are you as the big brother or sister? Who are you as a friend, husband, wife, manager, or parent? The complexity and depth of this identity development continues to generate volumes of studies, including recent books on the role of siblings, birth order, and emotional intelligence.

Educational System

Our school experiences largely affect how we think about learning throughout our lives. Walk into a kindergarten class and look around the room. It is a museum of artistic potential. A showcase of uninhibited expression and raw talent plasters the walls in a colorful exposition to rival any fall in New England. Seated in straight little rows are the artists—each at his or her own desk. Squirming, smiling, and barely able to contain all that energy, they eagerly await the next assignment. "How many artists do we have in here?" you ask. Every hand goes straight up without hesitation. "Me, me, call on me," they seem to cry out. But this is the first week of school. During the next few months, things will slowly change.

As the days pass, children will be taught to line up, raise their hands, wait for permission, and conform their activities to an acceptable norm. We will educate them to be conformists who work quietly, stay within the lines, and compete for the gold stars and teachers' praise. "Make your grass green," the teacher will advise them. "Color it right," the teacher will admonish, as if there were a right way to see the world. "Look at how Bill is doing his picture, Bonnie." Conform to the group. The teacher will pick the role models, teach us to compare ourselves, and create competitiveness even in our self-expression. Leaders and followers will be chosen based upon the teacher's prejudice. "You will not draw those pictures in my classroom." Failure to cooperate will be punishable by death—death of individuality, at least.

Research by T. E. Amiable shows that expectations by parents and teachers are significant in determining creativity. Teacher attitudes, historically, expected men to be more creative than women as well as more disruptive. Other findings found children who are encouraged and supported in their creative efforts continue striving toward higher creative efforts. Conversely, creativity is inhibited in tightly structured classrooms, and when students are grouped by ability only the higher ability students are benefited.[1]

Classically, education has been focused on teaching that emphasizes logic, analysis, argumentation, and fact. Specifically, these items include:

1. Observation and attention. This science model is characterized by objective observation. This separating model discounts the influence your subjective nature has upon your viewing and fosters a false sense of separateness and objectivity that does not awaken the nature of your co-creative mind.

2. Memorizing and regurgitation of facts. This approach assumes too often that the answer is already known and we simply have to learn the answers to gain both knowledge and understanding. Frequently, however, what is presented as factual is, in fact, culturally biased opinion, which is ideologically limited in both scope and content.

---

[1] Linda Perigo Moore, *You're Smarter Than You Think* (New York: Holt, Rinehart and Winston, 1985), page 37.

I recall the first time a Native American explained to me that Columbus did not discover America. America had been discovered thousands of years earlier by his people. Rather, the natives found Columbus wandering around their home. This perspective was decidedly in opposition to any previous facts I had been taught.

3. Analysis and judgment. Using a logical model of Aristotelian descent, we are asked to apply deduction or reasoning to an event or process and then present a compelling argument as to why our answer is correct. This approach favors those people who argue best.

Historically, schools have failed to teach us how new ideas are created and that we can contribute to that list. We do not learn that we can maximize our thinking power by using performance-enhancement techniques. We are not instructed in how our brain assimilates information visually, auditorily, and kinesthetically and how, although we might favor one of these areas, we can and should learn to utilize other areas. No one explains how to transfer learning from one area to another. No one mentions how we form our opinions and how those opinions can limit or empower our performance. No one gives us instruction in how different study techniques can maximize our learning, how we can problem solve using creative generation techniques, and how practicing self-motivating techniques can enhance our performance.

Learning could be presented as a process that involves all of our senses. Learning could be acknowledged as being based upon information that is often changing along with our changing understanding of that information. We could focus more on the processes of how we learn, so the value and practice can become lifelong traits that encourage self-learning as a valuable practice.

Historically, education has been results-oriented. For a few years in the evenings, I taught college. One of the questions most often asked in the first few minutes of the first night in class was, "Mr. Eiffert, what do I have to do to get an A in this class?" Clearly the educational system had taught the students to focus more on the grade, or outcome, of their educational experience than the experience itself. Students were not in school to learn; they were in school to graduate.

One of my responsibilities as a professor was to provide each student with a syllabus that spelled out my expectations—and hence my guidelines for getting that A. Among the classes I taught was a course entitled Creative Thinking. This course broke many of the rules and was intended to get students outside their safe area—to think on their own. In this class, my syllabus was intentionally vague. Now, when a student would ask me that first evening what she or he was expected to do for an A, I had the perfect response. "When you can figure out what you have to do to get an A," I would tell them, "you get the A."

It was amazing how many young, bright, talented students were confused or angered with my response. Some even went so far as to complain to other teachers or the department head that "Mr. Eiffert wasn't fair." I was not interested in giving students a right answer against which they could compare their answer; rather, I wanted them to look for a right answer of their own. I wanted to prepare students to make decisions based upon changing conditions. I wanted them to become comfortable trusting their own resources. I wanted them to develop divergent thinking skills, rather than simply convergent thinking skills. Most students, when they discovered that ambiguity, anxiety, and non-specific expectations were part of the program, became more comfortable with the course—and over a period of weeks often changed their attitudes dramatically.

Several of my students over the years have told me they learned more in my class about how to use what they knew than most other classes they took in college. The class prepared them for what they would actually encounter in the real world. I can live with that grade.

Conformity

When you think and feel as everyone else in the group you behave normally. This makes you feel a part of the group, even if somewhere inside of you there is a stirring of doubt. Society pressures us to conform. In Communist Russia, early dissidents were believed to be insane because they did not accept and conform with the beliefs of the group. This attitude is not new. It has occurred in many periods throughout history.

When you find yourself not in agreement with the conditioned, cultural response of the group, you are ill-at-ease with your feelings. Sometimes you find yourself questioning your thinking. Why do I feel differently? Why do I feel apart from the group? Is something wrong with me? Am I normal?

It is normal when one allows oneself time for reflection to have original and creative thoughts that may be out of agreement with the group. It is important not to confuse average thinking with normal thinking. Average thinking is primarily preoccupied with controlling and getting security and tangible things. Normal thinking at the creative or formative mind level seeks ways of expressing and being, which may or may not conform to the group.

Our hypnosis has been conditioned through habit, force, repetition, guilt, and emotional bribery. Go along with the group, and you will be happy-ever-after. But you must conform your behavior and your thoughts. You must aspire within the borders of acceptability. "No, you can't be a guitarist for Metallica when you grow up. You should be a lawyer." "No, you can't be a poet like Alan Ginsberg. You'll never make any money." Conform and be safe.

Conformity does not, however, bring either safety or happiness. It only masks your true identity. When your collective hypnosis blinds you to your identity and nature as a fully functioning person, you have lost your childlike mind. Experiences become automatic; you are no longer alive. "Aliveness" means vitality, and vitality is a condition of robust awareness and positive expectation of ability. In order to become creative, you must awaken your original sense of being alive.

Process

Imagine the final minutes of an exciting adventure film. The villain dangles perilously at the edge of a sheer cliff, suspended over a flaming volcano. The hero reaches out his hand, extending it beyond the edge as far as possible. The villain, one hand clinging to a crumbling rock, the other clutching a large bag, attempts to pull himself to safety. The hero calls out, "Drop the bag; take my hand." The villain looks at the hero, then to the bag. The bag is bursting with rare gems and gold. He hesitates, unable to let go of the bag, and shakes his head no. Faced with the decision to let go of the jewels and reach for safety, he cannot let go of his greed. His fingers slip, and the opportunity is missed. He falls into the volcano.

Clinging to what we already have is not just the folly of the villain. It is the bane of most adults. Once we have something, we are resistant to let it go—even for the opportunity of gaining something better. Higher gain, however, frequently asks us to surrender what we are holding in order to get something new—an attitude, an idea, a prejudice. This is a principle of process.

Surrendering or unlearning is a prerequisite for generating new patterns and releasing your creativity. In order to learn something new, you must first unlearn something old. In order to create a new mental pattern, you must allow your mind to be like that of the child. You must go back to that state where you were able to develop new thinking patterns and develop new possibilities, attitudes, and behaviors. Admitting you do not know or that your old answer might not work creates a vacuum into which new ideas can rush. To gain new insights and better ideas, you must release limiting assumptions, attitudes, or perceptions. Because it is unnatural for your brain to do this, you will need a system to guide you through the process.

Step One: Identify the Ways Your Thinking and Responses Are Holding You Back

Normally, your brain is always seeking patterns learned from previous experiences or activities and then projecting them into new situations. To stop this process, you must first be aware that it is occurring. You must learn to observe yourself to become aware of those situations in which bad thinking habits are limiting your choices. Your journaling practice can reveal recurring patterns of thoughts and behaviors. When you recognize the habitual response, you can act to change it. Many teachers and coaches will tell you that often the most difficult part of teaching something new is getting the student to lose something old.

Your old attitudes, feeling, and thoughts bind you to your existing level of understanding and awareness. Often they feel comfortable even when they are unproductive which makes releasing them difficult. New ideas, however, because they are not familiar, can often initially feel uncomfortable even when they are working. Failing to accept these feelings and advance in spite of them can hold you to lower performance outcomes. Often you know that a change would produce better results, and you still allow feelings of discomfort to hold you back from increasing your performance. Identifying these feelings and their associated limiting thinking, or negative assumptions in any situation, frequently reveals opportunities for creating new possibilities.

Consciously challenging your root metaphors, you compel your brain to begin the search for new patterns. You are then able to consciously choose to make these new changes and adaptations. Practicing cross-training techniques makes it possible to identify when your brain is operating under the influence of habitualized thought

processes. Gaining awareness means bringing the unconscious into the conscious and making the involuntary vol-
untary.

When you understand that the way you see something is simply your interpretation based upon historical
conditioning and is not right or wrong, you take the first
step in change. The perspective you hold is your interpretation of the outside event, and this creates your
experience on the inside. Becoming open to trying something new can change your interpretation. Remember,
you do not see the world the way it is—you see the world
the way you are.

Step Two: Try a New Way, Even if It Is Scary

Often one of the biggest fears of the learner is the fear of
appearing foolish. The ego is afraid of what the other
kids will say when you screw up, and we are all afraid we
are going to screw up because we have all done so in the
past. When you tried something new in fourth grade, you
screwed up, and everybody laughed at you. Becoming
psychologically safe is accepting the fact that even if
someone laughs at you, you are still OK. If you can
laugh along with them, it makes you feel even more safe.

Emotions strongly anchor your resistance to taking
any creative chances. To release those emotions, you must
consciously embrace the fear. Taking a leap of faith,
because you choose to expect all will turn out well,
requires great courage. Acknowledging fear, accepting
that it is part of the process of change, and moving forward regardless awakens strong feelings within you.
These powerful feelings help you to move past the discomfort your new ideas create and enable you to express
them anyway. Understanding that your new idea may not
withstand the test, yet moving forward in spite of the
doubt, releases your grade-school attitudes about learning and frees you for a more adult approach to your
thinking. Fully functioning people accept their uncertainty and self-doubt by challenging themselves and tak-

ing action. They have come to discover that these feelings and emotions are not real things, only sensations.

In weekly staff meetings, for example, perhaps you have felt uncomfortable speaking out and presenting your ideas in front of the group. You may discover in your journaling that this feeling is one that has carried over from an early age. You recall feeling uncomfortable speaking out in the classroom or at the dinner table. Although you may not know the cause of the feelings, they have accompanied you for so long that they are now predictable. The problem is, you often feel you have good ideas, which you fail to suggest. The frustration of this situation has become most uncomfortable for you. Yet, your fear of speaking out is even greater.

To change the situation, you realize you must first expect a better outcome by changing your approach. First you accept that it will be uncomfortable to speak out. You decide, however, you will no longer maintain your silence. You choose to wait for a moment when you have an idea you feel really confident about, and then you act. Whether you outline your thoughts first, write out your idea in detail, or simply ad-lib is unimportant; rather, it is the embracing of the fear and acting with confidence that will bring about the reward.

Journal Practice

Exploring Aspects of Your Self

On a blank piece of paper, draw a circle in the center of the page. Inside that circle, write your name. Now, as quickly as possible, create new circles radiating out of the center, each containing a word or words that describe a single aspect of your being—mother, teacher, athlete, thinker, cook, handyman, adviser, friend—words that describe who you are. Continue until you feel you have exhausted all the various possibilities of ways of describing your self.

Now pick one of the words you have written that describes who you are. On another clean sheet of paper, begin writing about that one aspect of yourself. Write openly and honestly, unedited, and with the knowledge that no one but you will ever see this piece of paper. Make a pact with yourself to tell all.

For example, I might write as Steve the son. I begin recalling my early childhood and then randomly weave my way through my early years living at home, growing up, leaving home, and considering what lies ahead as my parents age. There is no best way to do this, so simply begin. Whatever flows out of you is what you write. Do not edit yourself or leave something out that you find difficult. Put it all down. When you have finished, take a few minutes for a short walk. During the walk reflect and observe your thoughts as a result of this writing exercise, but do not analyze them too much. What thoughts come to your mind? How do you feel having finished the writing exercise?

When time permits, choose another aspect of your being and write about that concept. You may generate only a paragraph or two some days; other days you might write four or five pages. Write until you are satisfied you are finished. Then take your daily walk and relax.

As the process unfolds, think about the following things you may be learning about yourself:

→ Which aspects of yourself do you feel are out of balance?
→ Are there parts of you that have not been acknowledged?
→ Are there parts that are overtaxed?
→ Have you thought of any new aspects of yourself that you omitted when you created your original list? (You may add new aspects when you think of them.)
→ How do you see your future as different from your past?

3

The life you lead is the life you create. We experience our expectations.

"What the mind conceives, you can achieve."
—Oliver Wendell Holmes

Principle

I recall once waiting in line at a rental car counter at the airport in Phoenix. Four men ahead of me in line were told that for some reason the rental car agency had no record of their reservation. The young man at the counter was congenial, but unfortunately he had no other automobiles available at that time. The men all reacted to the event in different ways.

One man became belligerent, raising his voice and badgering the employee. A second man attempted to calm the first while pleading with the clerk to recheck his reservation list. This man seemed certain that somehow rechecking would sort out the problem.

The third man turned to the fourth and began saying how these things always seemed to plague him, that his life is a seeming list of problems and inconveniences every day. The fourth man looked around and noticed a rental counter down the concourse where there was no line. He left the group and walked to the counter, returning a moment later. He calmly explained to his colleagues that he had found a car available at the next counter that was cheaper than the original reservation.

Expectations Color Reactions to Events

All four men encountered the same event, yet each chose to express himself in a different way. The first two expected the clerk to solve their problem for them. The third expected the problem to be unsolvable. Only the fourth chose to solve the problem himself. Although none of the responses could be considered wrong, the fourth was clearly most constructive and provided the most pleasant experience.

Your world view, and as a result the life you experience, is bound to the paradigms that you use to understand what you believe you see happening in your world. Learning something new involves either incorporating the new information into an existing paradigm or developing a new paradigm.

Every situation contains both positive and negative elements. Asian cultures are typically more aware of this daily paradox than are western cultures. One example can be found in the Chinese character for crisis (see Figure 3-1), which represents both danger and opportunity. The individual who views the character must interpret the paradox and act appropriately. That person's perspective of the situation is the primary determinant of the outcome.

Figure 3-1   Chinese Character for Crisis

Sometimes what binds us to our limited thinking is the situation or context wherein we perceive a problem is occurring. Many situations are tied to areas that conceal your limitations and block your ability to see creative answers. An example of this characteristic is observing how easily we can often help another with a difficult decision or situation, yet in our own life we find a similar situation almost paralyzing. Frequently, these limitations occur in situations that are charged with emotion. We struggle—bound by our limitations—without realizing that a better solution may await us if we simply shift our perspective. Therein lies the paradox. The more involved or invested we are in a situation the less enabled we feel to solve it.

Your Thoughts Show Up in Your Experience

Have you ever wondered how someone attracts an experience? Most doctors have a few examples of what the medical field refers to as spontaneous healing. Because western medicine has not acknowledged these events as having medical validity, most physicians simply write these events off as flukes or oddities. More open-minded practitioners often classify them under the category of psychoneural healing.

While attending a workshop on mind-body relationships, I heard a neural psychologist relate the story of a woman who had severe rheumatoid arthritis. She had sought help from numerous physicians, none of whom had given her sustained relief. Now the disease was so advanced that she had lost the use of her hands and was unable to work at the hotel she owned. Exhausting all other possibilities, this woman began seeking alternative approaches.

Under hypnosis, and at a new physician's suggestion, the woman remembered a few years prior seeing an older woman and her two grandchildren checking into her hotel. She recalled how the two young people took exacting care of their grandmother, whose body was racked with advanced rheumatoid arthritis. She also recalled saying to herself that she wished someone would care for her as the two grandchildren obviously cared for their grandmother.

The physician concluded his story by explaining that following the hypnotherapy session and her revelation of the consequence of her thinking, the woman began a dramatic recovery of her affliction—and within six months, all traces of her arthritis were gone.

Stories of individuals attracting or healing their illnesses abound. I do not volunteer them to explore the medical applications; I am not a physician. I relate them to demonstrate the powerful, creative nature of our minds. Your ability to realize extraordinary outcomes from your thinking can be both positive and negative. Thoughts, whether conscious or unconscious, are powerful things. They create a reality for us by attracting an external experience to match with our internal expectation.

Negativity Begets Negativity

Of course, not all thoughts are of a healing nature. That negative attracts more negative is an obvious principle in mental action. Ideas attract like ideas. Like attracts like. Negative energy attracts more negative energy. Sufficient negativity can discharge even the most positive mental outlook.

We reduce the quality of our experience and outcomes when we expect less for ourselves. Lower expectations frequently limit the possibilities for us, obscuring them from our vision while simultaneously attracting the negative because we are looking for it. This principle of attraction is always at work, either consciously or unconsciously in our lives. When you expect less, you limit yourself.

Limitations in your thinking are either self-imposed or learned from those who influenced you most. Parents do not set out to limit children, but they often do. "You can't be an astronaut, honey. You're a girl." "Son, you'll never be a baseball player." "If you go in the deep end, you'll drown." Little comments, endlessly made without thought to their damage, slowly carve away a child's expectation of higher performance.

Negative limitations accumulate as children begin to accept them as true. After all, as a child, didn't you believe those big adults knew more than you did? The process of limiting your belief in yourself begins when you lose or fail to develop a strong locus of self evaluation. Taking ownership of the negative attitudes and perceptions of others, you succumb to lower expectations and acquire self-doubt. At the same time children are learning to doubt themselves, they are seeing examples of heroic fictionalized characters on television and in movies. These larger-than-life characters seem more powerful, more capable, more attractive, and creative. These heroes do not make mistakes. Problems are resolved without difficulty. Issues are black-and-white. Happy endings always occur in 60 minutes. These idealized fantasies and dramas make us seem helpless and make our lives seem less meaningful by contrast. When you find yourself coming up short in comparison, you lose even more confidence in yourself. By doubting your unlimited potentials, you place boundaries on yourself. Mistakes become, in your mind, failures rather than part of the process. Fear of making mistakes limits creative expression and risk-taking.

Expectations put into place at home are reinforced by social and cultural influences. An insight into why much of our thinking is negative comes from a survey of the number of positive versus negative messages we receive daily. Numerous studies in areas ranging from media, education, parenting, and the workplace have produced surprisingly similar results. On average, six of every seven messages in the United States are negative.

It should not surprise you that you begin to express the same attitudes and opinions to which you are regularly subjected—especially when you are operating in an unconscious manner.

In the workplace, managers create limited performance by restricting individual authority and responsibility. Often, managers develop mindsets about types of employees and foster a self-fulfilling relationship of expecting less and creating the workplace they expect. Viewing people as job descriptions rather than people with creative potential encourages them to learn to do their jobs and leave their thinking at home.

Time and time again, I have seen talented young people working in dead-end jobs who leave those jobs for opportunities in new environments where they blossom into tremendous contributors. Perhaps you have heard their former managers make comments like, "Why couldn't they have performed like that here?" or, "Just wait, they'll blow it one of these days." These managers are conspirators in limiting the quality of creative thinking their organizations express.

At a seminar, I spoke with a trainer from a large national manufacturing company. She was lamenting that her employees were not doing the reading and training they had been assigned. I told her of the new interactive training being done by companies such as the Ford Motor Company and WalMart. I described how these training models were both entertaining and experiential and how many companies were reporting dramatic training improvements with these models. She retorted that "her average laborer was nearly illiterate and would be phobic of even placing a long-distance phone call." I honestly believe she was unaware of how her assumed thinking limited her organization.

We Like to "Think About It"

One example of the subtle power of our limited thinking is the simple expression, "Let me think about it." Although no one would argue the value of thought, people constantly misuse the expression and limit their creative discovery.

An artist friend of mine needed to replace the doors on his garage. He thought about this project for several months, and each time he began thinking about doing it, he talked himself out of action because in his mind it seemed too overwhelming. Finally, one day he picked up a crowbar and began removing the old doors. Within a matter of hours, the new doors were installed and were wearing a fresh coat of paint. He told me later it was really easy to do once he quit thinking about it and just started doing something.

How often have you "thought yourself" out of creative action? How many times has your mind invented great obstacles to your imagined efforts and stopped your creative flow? How often have you found yourself thinking about something, only to discover that you were becoming emotionally involved with your thinking?

"Thinking about" can generate emotions that disempower or dissuade us from taking action, when in fact action was the catalyst we needed to awaken our creativity. In some cultures, the expression "think about" does not exist. The nearest expression to "think about" might be called "try see," which implies something vastly different.

"Try see" means to try and see what happens from your effort. Perhaps the words "try see" should be introduced into our vocabulary. "Thinking about" presupposes that your mental model will mimic the experience of direct action. "Try see" enables you to discover the nature of an idea or a thought by direct action in its behalf. This limitation of misusing "think about" is a construct of our western mental model—and is a construct shared with most members of our culture.

In life, action reveals new opportunities and creates its own inertia. Direct action leads to discovery, which creates new possibilities leading to more discovery, and so on. Action creates the positive feelings that stimulate us to go on. Thinking about action often stimulates false emotions and anxious feelings that can immobilize us, but I do not mean to devalue the role of thinking.

Thinking plays an important role in the creative process. Learning to think about how we are thinking can make us aware of when and how to use our mental processes to improve our creative expression. Productive thinking is inspirational, just as constructive action can be transformational.

Self-Limitations

Any animal can be trained to limit itself. Fleas, for example, are trained to jump in very specific ways. People are no different. They limit their lives with self-doubt, negative assumptions, and false beliefs. This limited thinking effects our relationships with our friends, families, and coworkers. Your personal and professional lives only expand as far as the chains of your expectations allow. As adults, people can make changes to release themselves from their assumed limitations; however, too often the assumptions are held so deep in the unconscious that they are difficult to identify.

British brain researcher Tony Buzan writes, ". . . when we describe ourselves as talented in certain areas and not talented in others, what we are really describing is those areas of our potential that we have successfully developed, and those areas of our potential that still lie dormant, which in reality could, with the right nurturing, flourish."[1] The "I can't," "It won't work," "I'm not good at this" thinking that many people constantly play in their heads programs them for negative experiences.

Martin Seligman, author of *Learned Optimism,* relates how individuals learn early to choose pessimistic or optimistic perspectives that govern their lives. Three thought and attitude characteristics are rooted in the learned pessimistic perspective:

---

[1] Tony Buzan, *Use Both Sides of Your Brain* (New York: Penguin Group, 1991), page 19.

1. Personalization. "Why is this happening to me?" The emphasis here is on the me, as if the individual is the only one to have ever had this problem.

2. Permanence. "This isn't going to get any better." This hopeless perspective is often a symptom of depression. The person is unable to see the possibilities because he or she is so encumbered by the problem.

3. Pervasiveness. "This kind of stuff always happens to me." This attitude that incidents are not random, but rather seem to choose an individual on purpose, creates more negative expectations.

Learned negative expectation is using your creativity to attract negative experiences. Attitudes that negatively affect your decisions and actions are based on long-standing habits, which actually demonstrate the power of your creative potential. The natural creativity you were born with has now been thwarted to limit life. Over time, you become oblivious to how your expectations have been shaped and how they limit your ability. Uncovering limitations and understanding that you emphasize what you focus upon are important first steps in discovering the impediments to your creative expression.

Process

It is important that you are cautious with the thoughts you create and that you learn how to discharge those thoughts which undermine your greater creativity. Learning to choose your thinking is a lifelong task that is fundamental to maintaining a fully functional outlook, as well as improved happiness and higher performance.

Through cross-training, you seek to uncover the thoughts that are limiting your outcomes and replace them with those that can empower you. In cross-training practice, you initiate the possibility of change by expecting the highest and best outcome for yourself. Slowly, habit by habit and decision by decision, limitation becomes opportunity through the practice of conscious choice. Although you cannot control how everything turns out, you can control your experience.

Change Your Perspective

Every situation or occurrence holds within it the possibility of multiple interpretations. Often these interpretations are paradoxical; therefore, locating a second perspective may be as simple as reversing the way you interpret the first. Learning to address situations at this level, rather than reacting to events unconsciously, enables you to begin seeing multiple outcomes.

Remember the Mark Twain character Tom Sawyer, who is told by his aunt that he cannot play until the fence is whitewashed? How does Tom interpret that statement? Does he accept the implied limitation that he must do the work, or does he reverse the statement by recasting the problem as an opportunity for delegation? "How can I get the fence whitewashed?" Tom asks himself. Tom reinvents the problem as an opportunity by shifting his emphasis from the limitation and onto the opportunity.

Changing your perspective and considering alternative interpretations or approaches by shifting the context in which you are seeing the problem often releases you from your initial interpretation and frees you to see alternative interpretations and solutions. We call this exercise *context shifting*. Context shifting enables you to disassociate from the personalization of the event. Context shifting moves the emphasis from one aspect of the issue to some other aspect, and in doing so releases opportunity thinking. Rather than redefining the problem, you are redefining the circumstances, the situation, or the perspective. By changing these backgrounds, you often shift your paradigms, the mindset within which you are viewing a situation.

Changing a paradigm can be as simple as consciously choosing to look for a second perspective. Creating a positive thought for every negative thought you hold is a simple, but powerful, exercise. Before you automatically respond in any situation where your first perception is negative, recognize your pattern—then consciously choose a corresponding positive thought to balance or harmonize your perspective. Over time and with practice, you might begin looking for two positives for every one negative. If you are an overly positive individual, you might reverse the process. The purpose is not to be either overly positive or negative, but rather to be aware of how you choose your responses and that you have a choice in the process that creates them.

The result of this thinking is not "Pollyannaism," but rather it is becoming consciously aware of how you are controlling your perceptions and how you can use your power to change them. Changing a negative pattern of reacting by using your conscious mind to uncover and address unconscious limitations awakens your creative, formative mind, transforming your perception of events.

Create Positive Expectation

Thomas Edison had the extraordinary honor of applying for more patents than any other American—1,093. From the light bulb to motion pictures, we enjoy daily the fruits of his creativity. Edison was not limited by the fear of failure. Like most scientists, he saw failure as a natural step toward success. Most of Edison's 1,093 inventions never saw commercial success. We do not remember those failures. We instead remember his successes. Can you say the same for yourself? How different would your life be if you saw failure as a by-product of the process in your route to success?

Nothing improves the moment more than an attitude of positive expectation. This concept collaborates with the world to bring you a better present. Creating an expectation of positive outcomes is perhaps the most rewarding use of your creative mind. If you are unaccustomed to expecting the positive, do not expect immediate results. You may have years of experience at being negative. Change may come slowly at first.

If you find yourself falling into a self-defeating, pessimistic world view, you must start by "depersonalizing" events and separating them from your feelings. Eliminating the "me" in these statements is one method of shifting how you are thinking about a situation. Rephrasing your internal dialogue to, "Why is this happening?" instead of, "Why is this happening to me?" results in a less personalizing statement that often enables the mind to see opportunities instead of problems. Practicing this form of attitude shifting can be very effective in teaching you new thinking and feeling styles that reveal more constructive possibilities.

For example, it is easy to fall into the trap of personalizing other people's behaviors. Perhaps a good friend seems cross and irritable with you at work. She skips your usual break together and fails to call you to explain why. You feel snubbed.

If you hold the pessimistic assumption that your friend is angry with you, then you believe the problem is about you. This situation is personalization. If, however, you shift your context so your focus is upon your friend, then you open your mind to the possibility that something unconnected to you may be influencing your friend's behavior. Perhaps your friend's problem has nothing to do with you. Now your emphasis can focus on how you can be helpful to him or her.

Choosing a more positive attitude of expectation creates the foundation for the next step—positive outcomes. You are now able to take a positive step toward finding solutions to problems. Once you consciously set out to positively change your attitude about one issue, it is a simple step to begin repeating the process with other issues. Although initially you may find yourself somewhat reluctant to accept a positive spin on something, the more you practice doing so, the more easily it comes to you. Practicing mental flexibility with your perspectives breaks the pervasive cycle of negative thinking. The more you play this game of mental substitution, the more you generate new thinking.

It is a universal principle of the nature of change that small positives create bigger positives, just as small negatives create bigger negatives. The little, day-to-day choices lead to the larger life events because you are patterning yourself toward them. You must understand than even the smallest positive act brings about positive changes, while even the smallest acts of negativity block you from higher attainment. Consciously cross-training your thinking improves your experience and increases your effectiveness and ability to respond. With each step up—no matter how small—you enable yourself to discover and use higher levels of creativity.

Visualize Your Experience

A powerful technique for altering your expectations and outcomes is visualization. The process of visualization, or mental imaging, can release you from non-functioning mental habits by enabling you to project more effective ones. Using your mental energy to attract positive images into your life enables you to tap the transformational energy of your formative mind.

As personal performance enhancement tools, visualization and mental imagery have a wealth of references to support their effectiveness. Many professional athletes have used the power of visualization for improving their performance. Jack Nicklaus, a famous golfer, says he never hits a shot, not even in practice, without having a very sharp, in-focus picture of it in his head. Olympian Dwight Stones, tennis star Chris Evert Lloyd, and quarterback John Brodie all attribute their peak success to mental imagery. As Olympian Arnold Schwarzenegger states, "A pump when I picture the muscle I want is worth 10 with my mind drifting."[2]

---

[2] Michael Murphy, *The Future of the Body* (Los Angeles: Jeremy P. Tarcher, 1992), page 444.

By mentally visualizing new possibilities, you are able to become comfortable with the new ideas and see the potential benefits prior to putting these changes into action. Visualization can release your mind of negative thoughts, entertain possibilities for positive change, or begin the process of profound change in both the mind and body.

Organizations visualize just as individuals do. Today's corporate executive officers are expected to bring vision to their leadership. Companies draft vision statements. Organizations and their management are often referred to as visionary. Mary Kay Ash based her cosmetics company on a vision of women as their own bosses. The ability to set a vision and then bring it into reality is one of man's highest achievements. Consciously or unconsciously, all of us practice visualization all the time. Discovering how to use visualization positively can change your thinking, as well as your experience.

Consider a Shaman who, when events require, can mentally shift his or her shape into an animal or bird to accomplish his or her quest. A Shaman attempting to heal a fellow tribesman can, for example, visualize himself traveling down a deep dark hole into the earth, flying past the rocks and roots to a secret underground spring, where he sips the water and has an inspiration. Returning from this vision quest, he can take his inspiration to the tribesman to create a healing incantation. Although this example may seem a bit far-fetched, it is very real to the participants. Frequently, the tribesmen recover. Who are we to doubt the structure of the thinking that achieved the goal, especially when it is built upon the same principles that we use to mentally visualize our success or failure everyday?

Visualization takes advantage of our physical, mental, and spiritual nature to create for us those things we desire in our lives. Although normally one would expect visualization to be used only in a positive way, negative visualization can produce negative results as well. When people see or imagine something bad occurring, without realizing it they often attract this negativity into their lives. Obviously, one should always use visualization in a positive way—visualizing only the best for all concerned. But surprisingly, we often do not. Too often we imagine the worst or project our fears into mental situations. It is important that you begin cross-training your mind to guard against seeing negative situations occurring or picturing bad or harmful outcomes. Although you can consider all the possibilities both good and bad when using critical thinking, you should never visualize the worst and see it happen to you. To begin using visualization more positively in your mental work, begin practicing using the following guidelines:

→ Find a quiet place.
→ Sit comfortably with your feet flat on the floor and hands folded in your lap.
→ Breathing through your nose, take a few deep breaths and begin relaxing the mind so you can form a clear image of what you want to achieve.
→ Be specific with your goal.
→ Create a clear mental picture or idea.
→ Use all your senses. If you are eating, taste the food in your mind. If you imagine that you are lying in the warm sun, feel the sun on your skin.
→ Be positive with your energy.
→ Focus on the mental picture frequently.
→ Maintain a sincere feeling about the practice.
→ Always conclude with the statement," I see this or something better for all concerned."

Although you cannot control life and those things that occur in your life, you can control yourself and learn to cooperate with the nature of how things happen. Success comes from your ability to flow more comfortably toward those positive experiences you wish to attract—and your ability to make the best of or avoid those events that you do not wish to attract. Visualization enables your mind to repeatedly see success and begin to believe it will occur. Practice prepares your mind to accept the new concept or pattern that it is given. When the event occurs, your mind will have already begun to formulate an expected pattern so the event can become consistent with your visualized world view. Visualization makes you more comfortable with attracting the positive, which empowers your thoughts and aligns your attitudes for positive action. Consciously preparing your mind to look for the positive outcome in the event and seeking the optimistic course, you begin to find your actions and deeds responding in a like manner.

Affirmations

Affirmations operate on the same principle as visualization. By affirming positive beliefs and expectations, you can work with your unconscious to attract these conditions into your life. Affirmations are a form of positive self-talk, a practice that is a hallmark of many high-performance individuals. Here are some guidelines for using affirmations to co-create desired outcomes.

1. Always state affirmations in the present tense: I am, I have, I possess, I express, etc. Acknowledge first that you already have what you are affirming.

2. Use active state, positive language: I am receiving, I am building, I am expressing. Do not choose the negative tense, as in "I no longer," or, "I will quit," etc.

3. State your affirmation simply. Use short, clear language.

4. Consult your feelings to assist you in creating the affirmations that are right for you.

5. No one else should be involved in setting these positive statements.

6. Repeat them often. When a moment presents itself, take a relaxing and peaceful pause and repeat your affirmations.

7. Write out your affirmations and date them. Initially, create no more than five affirmations with the final being a balancing, or harmonizing, statement.

8. Like visualization, always conclude with a statement that allows for possibilities you have not considered, such as, "This or something better," or, "I open myself to the divine mind to guide me in the best choice for all concerned."

Practice Exercises

1. **When your mind is moving toward pessimistic thinking or a negative mindset**

   Answer these questions the next time you find you are blaming yourself for an event:

   → Is it really my fault?
   → Do I assume blame too often or too easily?
   → Could this have happened to somebody else?
   → What am I focusing on that results in this negative feeling?
   → Is this a pattern that I recognize as having occurred in the past?
   → How would (insert someone whom you perceive as optimistic) see this event?
   → What new possibilities or better life event could this event now make possible?

   Answer these questions the next time you find you are personalizing the behavior of another person:

   → What, other than my actions, could cause him to act that way?
   → How could I help him?
   → I think her style is not conducive to healthy relationships with my style. Does she have this problem with others?
   → He is way too abrasive toward me. Is he this way with others?
   → They are mistaken about this issue, and I am confident I can find some evidence and present it in such a way that I can cause them to see things differently. Whom can I choose to help me with this issue?

   Consider the following questions when you find yourself stuck in an emotional situation:

   → Having this conversation (when we are getting

ready for work) is probably not a good idea. When could we have a more constructive meeting on this issue?

→ I think I need to get out of the office for a few (hours, days) to get some perspective here. Where could I go to clear my head?

→ The pressure at work right now is not allowing me to think clearly. What could I do to relieve some of this mental pressure?

2. **Try-See**

   Set aside time each week to try-see creative impulses you have. Avoid thinking about these creative impulses too much until you have the time to work them out. Give them over to your unconscious mind by saying to yourself, "I will solve this later in the week at my try-see session."

3. **Positive Self-Talk**

   Practice reversing your disempowering self-talk language into a more positive tone. Substitute a negative thought or expectation with a positive thought or expectation.

4. **Visualization**

   Select three areas in your life where you believe visualization could improve your performance or experience. Set aside 10 minutes each day to work on any one of those three areas you have identified. At the end of two weeks, sit down and write about any progress you have seen in that area. When you are satisfied with your improvement, choose the second of your three areas and begin working on it.

5. **Affirmation Exercise**

   Lie in a comfortable position. As you slow your breathing and relax, allow your mind to search the body for any areas of tension and consciously relax those areas. Deepen your breathing to your lower diaphragm at the base of your navel. Exhale slowly until your lungs seem completely deflated and then allow the inhalation to occur spontaneously. Feel the bellows of your lungs expand from front and back, side to side. Begin slowly saying and seeing your affirmations, energizing them with your belief that the affirmation is already true in your life. Repeat each affirmation up to five times.

Act in your daily life as if the affirmations had already created the reality in your life. See and believe yourself already receiving the things you have affirmed.

Journal Practice

Revealing the Negative in Your Life

1. Keep a record of positive and negative information that you encounter. Consciously begin looking for and recording it.

2. Look particularly at newscasts on television and count the number of negative stories and the positive stories.

3. Begin to record your own perceptions throughout the day. How often do you think or say, " I don't like something," or, " I can't," or, "It will never work," and so on. Do your negative perceptions and unmotivating messages exceed your positive ones?

4. Record those times you have talked yourself out of some new idea or impulse. Say, for example, you were invited to go roller skating with a group of friends one evening. You had not roller skated since junior high school and recalled that it was not a positive experience. Thinking about skating, you became uneasy. You decide to decline the offer.

5. Replay an event where you allowed negative thinking to undermine your creativity. Rewrite the event, imagining you had taken a more positive position.

4

We function best when approaching life with our whole brains.

"Give your brain as much attention as you do your hair, and you'll be 1,000 times better off."
—Malcolm X

Principle

Who is reading this book? Is it you? Which you? A current theory of many psychologists and educators is that we have many different minds, or manifestations of our minds. Perhaps different environments produce different pattern-recognizing behaviors. Many people might agree that they tend to be different people in different situations.

When I asked you the question, "Who thinks about it?", do you have a clear image of your perceived I, the thinker behind your eyes, the little person in your head?

53

If you asked yourself, "I wonder what he means by that?", who is asking you the question? The hemisphere where this type of thinking occurs, the one with which most of us frequently identify, is the left hemisphere. It is where the "I" most of us perceive ourselves to be resides. This "I" is a manifestation of your left-side thinking.

We all have two hemispheres in our brain. In most human brains, the left hemisphere is specialized in what we consider linear, or logical, thinking. The right side is our non-logical, pattern-making brain. Figure 4-1 describes the functions of the hemispheres in more detail. Keep in mind that in approximately 15 percent of the population who are either left-handed, dyslexic, or reverse hemisphere, the geographic placement may be reversed. Consequently, the processes and signaling in which the two hemispheres work is not consistent with the other 85 percent of the population.

The Right Hemisphere

Most children are born right hemisphere-dominant. This right side dominance is more useful as they shape events into patterns during their discovery of the world. Children at their earliest learning stages respond to familiar shapes, smells, and sounds—all strong right pattern-associating behaviors. As they grow and the connection between the two hemispheres develops, they begin to demonstrate stronger cognitive skills as right hemisphere functions move to the left. During this period of transference and development, specific functions localize themselves within geographic areas. Children have much greater mental elasticity for movement between hemispheres if need be than do adults. As we age, our mental functions tend to become more localized into specific areas and relocating them becomes increasingly difficult, if not impossible.

Figure 4-1   Left Hemisphere and Right Hemisphere

Left Hemisphere	*Right Hemisphere*
one-at-a-time	all-at-once
sequential	simultaneous-complex
detail-focused	holistic; big picture
abstracts the world to bits and pieces	connects the pieces
logical: cause and effect	analogistic; sees things as representative
seeks facts and verification	qualitative; feelings
thought through information	thought through emotion
linear thinking	imagistic thinking
rule-governed	transformative
looks to previously learned information	creates new patterns
verbal talks uses syntax, grammar	words as sounds, mute cannot create language
remembers complex motor sequences	remembers complex images
knows how	discovers what
recognizes symbols and old patterns	designs new symbols and new patterns
Black and white	color
Slow thinking	instant knowing
Rational	Intuitive

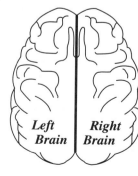

Left Brain   *Right Brain*

The right hemisphere is the source of our intuition, insight, metaphor, imagination—and perhaps collective memory. Right mental processes are sensory, involving more feelings as part of the processing. The right side does not perceive the "I" at the moment of the experience. Its instantaneous processing does not allow time for separating distinctions. Right-side experiences occur all at once, in complete detail, and do not seem to be bound by time and space.

This hemisphere is heavily involved in the creative process. The right hemisphere provides us pattern-generating and shaping activity and searches for new or richer meanings. This hemisphere must be stimulated in the first stages of the creative process.

Playfulness is a characteristic of the right brain. It also is a characteristic we identified with highly creative people in Chapter 1, which described the elements of creativity. Playing stimulates the right hemisphere and enables the mind to see new patterns in the familiar, or new opportunities where before none existed. Original thoughts and ideas are formed when the mind of creative discovery and imagination is so engaged.

Rather than wasted time, play and even idleness is often very beneficial behavior. Nearly everyone has experienced those moments when a calm, relaxed, unfocused mind seems to effortlessly solve problems, generate ideas, or deal with complex situations. Once we have experienced this right hemisphere's creative flowing, we are strongly interested in discovering ways to recreate the event.

Although most people are familiar with the names of many of the great thinkers of the past, few of us are familiar with how these thinkers gained their insights and inspiration for their theories and discoveries. Research into the process of these mental giants points to a process of focused inquiry followed by unfocused relaxation. In other words, it is intense work followed by mental play. "The final breakthrough in every recorded case," writes Joseph C. Pearce in *The Crack in the Cosmic Egg*, "occurs at a moment when the logical processes have been momentarily suspended, a moment of relaxation from serious work."[1] Einstein has written that many of his best ideas came while dreaming or shaving. Edison was noted for slipping into a deep reverie from which he was not to be disturbed. The famous Greek playwright Euripides, while lounging in the bath, was struck with his famous displacement theory. Newton had many of his best ideas while cooling his heels at the farm caring for his mother. In each example, the insight did not come during the tension of concentration, although this step was necessary to prepare the mind; rather, the insight came at a moment when the mind was unfixed, often preoccupied with something totally unrelated to the question.

The Left Hemisphere

Left hemisphere processes are much slower. Left thinking is often seemingly devoid of emotion and is associated with more dissociated or objective processes. Left-sided thinking is more aware of the "I" in the process and often is perceived as more rational. Here also is the source of operations that deals with language, sequence, and organization. The left hemisphere makes judgments. This left hemisphere also perceives the temporal distinctions of past and future. The left hemisphere can create abstractions and is deeply involved in the process of finding the facts.

The left hemisphere often relies heavily on the process of intellect. Consider intellect as directly in contrast with creativity. Whereas intellect reduces to the specific, creative processes expand into larger referential contexts. It is this isolating nature of intellect that results in its not always functioning in the best interest of the whole.

Alan Watts, in *The Book*, observes that intelligence will never act with disregard to the well-being of the system—because intelligence always is directed toward

---

[1] Joseph Chilton Pearce, *A Crack in the Cosmic Egg* (New York: Julian Press, 1971), page 70.

survival of the whole. It is intelligence that will cause someone to risk his or her life to save the life of another person they do not even know. Intellect, on the other hand, because it separates the "I" from the collective, does not assume responsibility for its behavior and as a result can harm the group in the vain attempt to gain advantage for self. Intellect will build weapons of mass destruction without regard for the long-term consequences of its actions. Our left hemisphere tends to intellectualize, while our creative, formative right side is more associated with intelligence.

The confident judging left hemisphere is the one you must quiet in the early stages of the creative process. This logical reasoning mind should not be called upon until after the new idea or ideas have struck, much later in the creative process. Although both types of thinking are necessary for a fully functioning mental process, each has its appropriate time and place to maximize thinking performance. Because the left hemisphere is pattern-recognizing, it will tend to seek out those patterns it already recognizes. If your mind already thinks it knows, it sees little value in learning something new. Often the largest problem is keeping the critical left hemisphere quiet while the creative right is conjuring its insight.

In today's high-speed, high success-dominated society, too much emphasis is often placed on left-side functioning, which often satisfies immediate needs while generating results at the expense of longer term values and personal satisfaction. This bottom-line emphasis at the expense of well-being fails to reference the whole. Over-reliance on this left hemisphere thinking can actually produce physical and mental discomfort, because it is failing to acknowledge the value of other sensory data in disagreement with the analytical left. Balancing right hemisphere creative thinking into the process promotes a sense of greater well-being through its acknowledgment of broader considerations and long-term emphasis.

Whole-Brain Thinking

Research on the processes of bicameral functioning has revealed that the two hemispheres actually have two different experiences of the same events. Both sides use complex processes for thinking and problem solving. The verbal left demonstrates reductionistic, analytical, critical thinking, and the spatial right makes use of metaphorical, generative, big-picture thinking. It is the nature of these two separate hemispheres to often work in contradictory ways, resulting in the thinker being of two minds on an issue. This system enables us to understand the problems inherent in relying too heavily upon a single hemisphere's process for our decision-making. Cross-training suggests that rather than either/or, with emphasis on choosing one over the other, we look to the paradox to explain a new definition that incorporates both thinking processes into the final equation.

Women, who tend to synthesize their thinking across a broad range of the brain, often utilize both brain hemispheres in concert when thinking and participating in activities. Men, conversely, tend to isolate disparate functions and activities into smaller areas of the individual hemispheres. Women's brains are oriented more to synthesizing, while men's brains are more compartmentalizing. It is these different mental processes that, in part, explain why the sexes think and perceive differently.

When both sides of the mind become constructively engaged in the thinking, we refer to the process as whole-brain thinking. Whole-brain thinking is not a subject most of us have much experience in practicing.

In the Zen tradition, the left mind is associated with the process of thinking, while the right mind is associated with the process of knowing. When we consciously move into our right mind, we not only find our creativity enhanced, but we also discover the same information being presented in non-logical ways. This discovery creates a more comprehensive understanding of the information being presented and the realization of possibilities that exist in every circumstance. When the creative thinking process is desired, it becomes necessary for you to actively engage the right mind and subdue the left. Consciously shifting to your creative-thinking right mind requires specific practices that can predictably affect this mental transference. Anyone can do it. All it requires is a little practice in cross-training.

Process

Maximizing our creativity comes from the ability to move from left to right dominance when the need arises. This ability is not normally a routine practice of most people, and success requires specific cross-training skills and some practice. Initially, these techniques may seem difficult or unusual, but with experience and time you will discover that your thinking approach is beginning to change—and you are finding more creative ideas faster and with greater predictability.

Although your goal should be whole-brain thinking, the vast majority of us find ourselves stuck on the left side. You might want to start by taking the self-test "Which Side Are You On?" to determine which side of the brain you favor. The information that follows is focused on moving from the left to the right. If you find yourself leaning more naturally to the right, you might want to skip directly to the exercises designed to enhance left-brain thinking.

Which Side Are You On?

Are you a left-brained or a right-brained thinker? Strictly speaking, of course, you are both, because normal people use both sides of their brains for virtually everything they do. Nevertheless, many people think in a way that scientists associate with one or the other of the brain's hemispheres. To determine your own thinking style, try this just-for-fun questionnaire, prepared under the guidance of Ivan Muse, a professor of education at Brigham Young University. (Note: you will need a partner to help you with Section Three.)

Section One

1. When you go to a movie, do you prefer to sit
   a. On the left side of the theater
   b. On the right side of the theater
   c. In the center or no preference

2. Do you like to work
   a. On a team
   b. By yourself

3. When someone gives you an assignment, do you prefer
   a. Highly specific instructions
   b. Rather flexible instructions

4. Do you tend to make decisions
   a. On a gut feeling or hunch
   b. After careful analysis and thought

5. In general, do you feel that laws
   a. Should be strictly enforced for everyone
   b. Should be enforced only after considering individual circumstances

6. To motivate yourself, do you prefer
   a. Competing with yourself
   b. Competing with others

7. Which drawing is closest to the way you hold a pen?

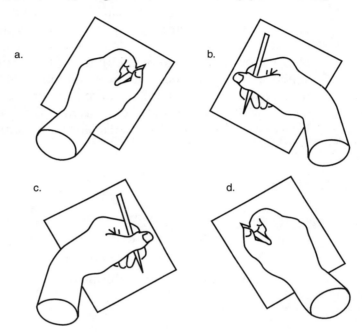

8. Which face seems happier to you?

   c. They seem the same.

9. Would you prefer to be married to someone who
   a. Has unusual ideas and daring concepts
   b. Is a thorough planner and organizer

10. When you shop, do you tend to buy
    a. After reading labels and comparing costs
    b. On impulse

11. Does daydreaming help you make decisions?
    a. Frequently
    b. Sometimes
    c. Rarely

12. Which makes you happiest?
    a. Doing a crossword puzzle
    b. Sketching or drawing
    c. Finishing a work assignment
    d. Singing in the shower

13. When you meet someone, is it easier to
    a. Remember the name
    b. Remember the face
    c. Both are equally easy or difficult

14. Pick the two adjectives that best describe how you work.
    a. Organized (efficient, orderly)
    b. Imaginative (good at thinking up new ideas)
    c. Outgoing (work well with others)
    d. Result-oriented (complete everything you start)
    e. Intellectual (use reasoning powers to solve tasks)
    f. Intuitive (reach conclusions by a "sixth-sense")

15. At a meeting, do you prefer
    a. A graphic slide presentation
    b. A dynamic speaker

16. When driving in a city that you know slightly, do you
    a. Get a map and ask for explicit directions
    b. Navigate by your own sense of direction

17. In a discussion, do you usually feel that
    a. There are clear right and wrong positions
    b. Both sides have merit

18. After attending a play or a movie, do you prefer
    a. To talk to others about it
    b. To think it over privately

19. When do you do your best work?
    a. Early in the morning
    b. Late in the afternoon or evening
    c. At no particular time of day

20. If chosen to be a leader, would you rather be known as
    a. Humane, understanding, and empathetic
    b. Logical, organized, and fair

Section Two

Here are four problems. Rank them in order of preference, with number one being the type of problem you most like to solve and number four being your least-favorite. (You do not need to answer the questions; although, the answers will be given for those who want them.)

Problem A

A grain company mixes seed costing 20 cents a pound with seed costing 25 cents a pound to produce a blend of seed costing 22 cents a pound. How many pounds of the more expensive seed are in a 50-pound sack of this mixture?

a. 20
b. 25
c. 30
d. 40
e. None of these

Problem B

You are confined to a prison cell that has two doors. One leads to freedom; the opposite one leads to instant death. You do not know which door is which. With you are two jailers. One of them always tells the truth; the other always lies. Again, you do not know who is who. You may ask either of the jailers—but not both—one question. What question should you ask to learn which door leads to freedom?

Problem C

Which of the following four cutouts could be folded in such a way that it produces the cube in the drawing?

Problem D

The words house, village, and thumb are all related to
the word green in that they combine with green in a
common word or phrase: greenhouse, village green,
green thumb. In each example below, find the word
that relates to all three:

a. blue, cake, cottage

b. water, pen, soda

c. up, book, charge

d. man, screen, sure

Section Three

For this section, you need a partner. Give the book to
your partner now and do not read the rest of these
instructions.

    Instructions for partner: Sit in front of the person
being examined and ask the 10 questions below. Pay no
attention to the answers, but watch the person's eyes to
see in which direction he first glances when mulling over
the problem. Put a check in the appropriate box below.
(He need not glance exactly to the side; if he glances up
and to his left, that is considered a leftward glance.) If he
does not look to either side, do not check either box.

	Left Glance	*Right Glance*
1. How many letters are there in the word California?		
2. A cube has how many points (i.e. pointed corners)?		
3. What was the name of your favorite grade school teacher?		
4. Multiply seven times 14 in your head.		

	Left Glance	**Right Glance**
5. Name the letters of the alphabet that have curves in their capital-letter forms.		
6. Give three meanings for the word pound.		
7. What color shirt (blouse) did you wear yesterday?		
8. How many doorways do you pass through going from the street to your bedroom?		
9. Name the letters of the alphabet that contain the sound ee.		
10. Which way does the profile of George Washington face on a quarter?		

Interpreting Questionnaire

Section One

Answers that tend to indicate a left-brain preference get five points each. Right-brain answers get one point. Answers that indicate no preference get three points each.

1. a=5   b=1   c=3

The theory here is that left-brained poeple may tend to sit on the left side of theaters so the screen will fall more into their right visual field, which sends information directly to the left hemisphere of the brain. For right-brainers, the situation is reversed.

2. a=1   b=5
3. a=5   b=1
4. a=1   b=5

The answer to question number four depends on the fact that right-brained people may be more likely to jump to emotional or intuitive conclusions, while left-brained people are usually more analytical.

5. a=5   b=1
6. a=1   b=5
7. a=1   b=5   c=5   d=1
8. a=5   b=1   c=3

Because the right hemisphere of the brain is usually more emotionally sensitive, most people see figure A as happier. Presumably this is because the smiling side of its mouth falls in the left visual field, which goes directly to the right hemisphere.

9. a=1   b=5
10. a=5   b=1
11. a=1   b=3   c=5
12. a=5   b=1   c=5   d=1
13. a=5   b=1   c=3

Left-brained people tend to be better at remembering names than faces. For right-brainers, the reverse is true.

14. a=5   b=1   c=1   d=5   e=5   f=1
15. a=1   b=5
16. a=5   b=1

Left-brainers usually want explicit directions, while right-brainers regard asking for directions as an admission of failure.

17.   a=5   b=1
18.   a=5   b=1
19.   a=5   b=1   c=3
20.   a=1   b=5

Section Two

Problems A and B are left-brain problems because they involve mathematics and logic, respectively. The other two are right-brained, because they depend on visualizing a folded figure (problem C) or thinking of imaginative connections between words (problem D). Score this section according to which two problems you preferred to do. Find your score in the table below:

Problem ranked number one

	A	B	C	D
A	–	15	11	11
B	15	–	11	11
C	7	7	–	3
D	7	7	3	–

Answers to Section Two

Problem A: a. 20 pounds

Problem B: Ask either jailer, "If I asked the other jailer to point to the door to freedom, which door would he point to?" Then go through the door opposite the one the jailer indicates. If you put the question to the truthful jailer, he will honestly tell you what the other jailer would have said—that is, a lie. If you ask the lying jailer, he will lie and tell you the opposite of what the truthful jailer would have said.

Problem C: b.

Problem D: a. cheese; b. fountain; c. cover; d. fire

Section Three

Some studies have suggested that people glance in the directon opposite to the hemisphere that is most active at the time. That is, a person who looks to his left may be using his right hemisphere, and vice-versa. So give yourself one point for every left glance, five points for every right glance, and three points for each pair of boxes that your tester left unchecked.

Add your scores for sections one, two, and three together. If the total is between 34 and 85 points, you have shown a preference for right-brain thinking. You may have creative, musical, or artistic talents. You often rely on feelings and intuition in making decisions. You are good at spotting overall patterns based on limited evidence and excel at solving complex problems that demand a creative and insightful approach. You detest dealing with messy details.

If you scored between 119 and 170 points, you have demonstrated a preference for left-brain thinking. You are likely to be a verbal, logical, analytical person, perhaps with mathematical skills. You are meticulous and well-organized and excel at activities that require careful planning, cost projections, and attention to detail. You would rather see one project carried through to completion than six half-finished.

If you scored between 86 and 118 points, you have indicated that you use both right-brain and left-brain thinking equally.

Seek Out New Experiences

The pattern-making right is open to creating new patterns or creating new ways to derive understanding from existing patterns. Doing things you have never done before, working in or experiencing unfamiliar terrain, or being exposed to ideas from new perspectives can all create new thought patterns that enable you to see the world in new and different ways. It is this new pattern-making process that inspires ideas and innovation both at work and at play.

Many organizations rotate managers into departments about which they know nothing. It is amazing the possibilities that occur when someone who has not learned the right and wrong way attempts problem solving. Research indicates that the most successful managers have been rotated in this manner an average of nearly four times in their careers. Placing them in situations where they have few pre-existing patterns inspires the use of their right brain's pattern-making and holistic thinking skills. This often results in some new innovation that the left hemisphere's "We already know how to do it" brain might fail to see.

Recently at a business conference, a senior manager told me her company had been cycling management staff into new departments for one year to cross-train their brains. I ask her what the consensus was. "Everybody is a little scared and a lot excited," she replied. "It is impacting everything we do. We're really having fun. But it has also been productive to the company." Wouldn't it be wonderful if we all suddenly rediscovered that having some fun in the workplace could also be productive?

Relax Your Mind

Any activity that stimulates your mind to release its fixed perspectives and relax seems to be effective in stimulating this generative state of right-mindedness. Stop trying to have a creative idea. Instead, move into a state of creative consciousness that enables you to have the creative idea.

I have asked thousands of people what they were doing when they came up with their brilliant ideas. Not surprisingly, the results have been remarkably consistent. Here are the top four:

1. "Driving in my car." Astrophysicist Steven Weinberg had a sudden insight into the unified field theory while driving his car to the Massachusetts Institute of Technology one day. It is easy to become preoccupied with your thoughts while driving. I suppose this situation indicates just how little of our conscious minds we often engage while driving. Our mind, bored with the trivial task of driving, looks for other ways to entertain itself. The right hemisphere begins the process of stringing, where one idea triggers another and then another, and so on. Does this sound familiar?

Wonder what we'll fix for dinner tonight? It needs to be something quick. Maybe I should get some takeout? That would play hell with my waistline. Why can't I seem to lose any weight? Maybe I need to go on a diet. What I really need is to exercise. Hey, I could buy one of those exercise bikes. Perhaps this winter. Right now I'd really rather walk outside. I wish I could exercise outside in our neighborhood. We don't have any sidewalks. I'd feel funny in our neighborhood walking down the street. If only I could find a place in the country. My wife and I love to garden. I wonder if she remembered the dry cleaning? Boy, I wish we'd bought those cell phones.

Does this random thinking pattern sound like the type of self-talk you sometimes engage in when driving your car? If you recognize this style of thinking as one you have experienced when driving, then you know driving is stimulating your right hemisphere.

This style of thinking is sometimes termed lateral thinking. Patterns of relationships are generated from seemingly random topics, with none of them being developed into any detail. Generating new patterns in this almost skipping manner triggers new routes for our thinking to follow. These new information routes often cause us to associate or combine thoughts in a new way and result in the insights or breakthrough ideas we suddenly experience.

2. "When I'm exercising or walking." Physicist Werner Heisenberg was distraught, and his health was challenged. He was in a quandary regarding the obvious contradiction of the wave-particle paradox. One evening, his anguish too great, he went for an evening walk in the park across from his home. Suddenly he had an insight, which completely and instantly explained the contradiction. It was the breakthrough in physics we now know as the Uncertainty Principle.

Aristotle called walking the sport of genius. Although your exercise choice may vary, the process is what is important. Research has shown that aerobic activity increases the flow of blood and oxygen to the brain, resulting in greater mental alertness and proficiency. Some studies show an increase of 10 to 12 percent in mental proficiency after a regular schedule of aerobic exercise over a period of a few weeks. Physical movements also stimulate our thinking and can reroute thinking in new and previously unexperienced ways. Any form of movement that uses cross-lateralizing movement stimulates higher, more advanced thinking. Aerobic-type exercise also increases the metabolic rate, producing a natural sense of energy in the body. Finally, sustained aerobic exercise causes the body to produce endorphins—a feel-good chemical that stimulates the senses and accentuates our sense of well-being.

3. "When I am in the bathtub, shower, or swimming pool." The buoyancy of water enables muscles to relax when submerged. Even though you are not submerged in a shower, the stream of water has a massaging effect that relaxes your muscles and your mind. Also, hot water, like exercise, stimulates blood circulation.

Additionally, you and I are more than 90 percent liquid. Your brain is completely nestled in water, which is directly connected to the other fluid systems through your entire body. In the prenatal state you spent the first nine months of your life in the amphibious state. When you enter water, it transports you back to that prenatal "safe in the womb" mode.

Many people report they do not even have to be in the water to receive the effects. Sitting by the ocean, canoeing on a river, or sailing on a lake all seem to have the same generative effect on thinking.

4. "When drifting off to sleep at night or when I first awake in the morning." In this transitional zone where our mind is disengaging from its vigilant awareness, ideas seem to occur. Like daydreaming, this non-alert mental mode has much in common with meditation in its effects on our thinking. Although our bodies are in the restive state when we sleep, our minds are ever awake as they embark on the dream state. Dream states are altered consciousnesses that provide us access to information unavailable in ordinary moments. When you are awaking or are just drifting off to sleep, the line between these consciousness states is blurred—and you can often have insights through the mixed patterns created in this condition.

Practice Exercises

1. Right Hemisphere Exercises

a. Clustering

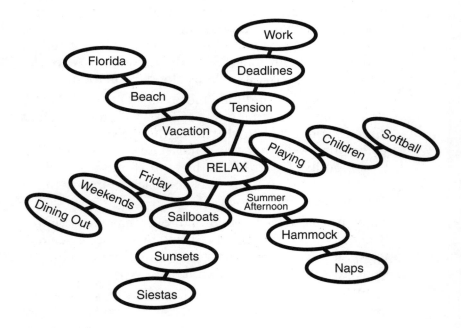

Locate a clean sheet of paper and a pencil or pen. Sit comfortably and allow your body to relax. Close your eyes and focus your mind on your breathing for a moment. Observe the breath slowly moving in and out. Now choose a nucleus word, any word that can have multiple interpretations.

Write the word down in the top center third of the page and circle it. Now begin immediately writing down words or concepts that flow from that word. Write quickly and circle each new word you think of radiating outward from the center. Connect new words with lines to the previous word that stimulated it. If a completely new idea or word comes to mind, go back to the central nucleus and begin working outward again.

Do not judge your ideas or censure them. Your right hemisphere is creating, and your left hemisphere may wish to doubt the validity of the process. Do not let the left hemisphere block the creative process.

Allow the flow to continue naturally and randomly, creating associated word connections as you feel they should be connected. If you occasionally have a pause, doodle with the connections, focusing upon your nucleus word and relaxed breathing until a new word is generated.

After a few minutes, most people feel the urge to stop clustering and begin writing about some idea or concept this technique has triggered in their heads. Sometimes the urge to write happens suddenly, and sometimes it occurs more slowly. Whatever the feeling, it will come with a sense that you now have something to write about.

You may wish to scan your cluster before writing or simply start. If you are unsure of what sentence to begin with, simply write whatever is in your head. Allow each subsequent sentence to flow naturally. Do not force it or think about it, but rather let the words flow into sentences and let the sentences flow into paragraphs.

At some point, you may feel that you are finished and want to simply stop the writing process. Usually no more than a page of writing is necessary to produce what writing instructor and author Gabriel Ricco calls a vignette. The process has opened up the design mind and often results in some interesting insights about the nucleus word. On occasion, you may wish to consciously look back at the initial core of elements that started your cluster and see whether you can fold the ideas you have written back to a full-circle close.

Read aloud what you have written. If you wish, you may now use your design mind to make changes or improvements on the writing until you feel that it is complete.

This process of clustering enables us to get in touch with our formative right mind. This design mind enables us to recast ideas in new forms and employ new patterns that release our creative expression.

b. Upside-Down Drawing

Observe the drawing at left. Do not turn the book around, but simply look at the inverted drawing. You will be making a drawing of this illustration by copying it just as it appears, upside down.

Find a quiet place where you will not be disturbed, and choose an oversize pad and soft lead pencil. Allow yourself several minutes for this exercise. You may wish to listen to some relaxing music, such as Handel's "Water Music" or Vivaldi's "Four Seasons." Allow your body to relax by focusing upon your breathing and letting the mind simply observe the drawing for a few moments.

You will begin to see as you look at the inverted illustration that the lines all fit together in patterns. Where one line ends, another begins. All the lines have certain angles that relate to other angles and also relate to the edge of the page. Within the shapes are spaces that also have specific patterns. Allow a moment for the patterns to become more comfortable.

Beginning at the top of the page, the bottom of the drawing, start copying the lines moving from one to another adjacent line at a comfortable pace. Observe how each connects with the next, how the angles are created, and how the forms align themselves with the page.

As your drawing progresses, you may notice that the music disappears and you become engrossed with how the various lines, angles and shapes are forming. Your left mind, having lost all interest in the event, has surrendered to the design right mind—and it is now engrossed in the capturing of this new pattern. Continue the process until you finish adding every line in the inverted drawing.

When you have completed the drawing, you may turn both the book and your drawing completely around. You will be surprised, especially if you have never thought yourself an artist, about how well your drawing turned out.

c. Word Play

Find one word that can be associated with all three of the following words: (Example: Money, strike, and weight are all descriptions of different meanings for the word pound.)

Tree, page, table

d. Draw the Answers to the Following Questions:

1. What's for lunch?
2. Is that your bike?
3. Where are you going on vacation?

2. Left Hemisphere Exercises

See how far you can progress through the alphabet in three minutes assigning names of fruits or vegetables to each letter. Example: Apple =a, banana = b, cherry = c, and so on. Try this exercise with other categories as well (names, cities, countries, animals, etc.)

Find the pattern in the following numbers:

62,60,62,66,64,66,70,68,70,74

5

Conditions are not emotions. How you feel about an event is not the event.

"Things may happen around you, and things may happen to you, but the only things that matter are the things that happen in you."
—Eric Butterworth, Unity minister

Principle

At the cellular level, the human brain looks and operates like the brains of many other animals. We are as much as 98 percent identical in our genetic and brain structures to an orangutan. Animals, however, are missing our advanced cerebral cortex development. The higher cognition and abstraction occurring in this larger cerebral cortex brain is unique to man. Much of what we consider ourselves to be resides inside this newer learning brain. This new brain is home to most of what we think of as our logical processes. Our self-concept, language, symbol-making, and analytical thinking processes dwell in this most recently developed brain.

The Limbic Brain and the Cerebral Cortex

Increasingly, the new brain is assuming more and more complex tasks. But try as it might, it can never fully separate itself from the influences of the older relatives. For all of our perceived evolution and sophistication, underneath the new brain still lies the limbic brain and reptilian brains, the primary operating system of our ancient ancestors. Our limbic brain, the emotional, instinctive, fight-or-flight brain coats our 21st-century thoughts with primordial feelings. Which brain you and I engage at any moment is decided by a neurological process called the *reticular activating system*, or RAS. The RAS engages our limbic brain when we are excited and our cerebral cortex when we relax.

Instantaneous mental processing does have value in our survival and contributes to the simplification of our lives. Mental habits help us complete certain processes quickly. Recognizing patterns and acting quickly is important to the process of survival in life-threatening situations. In many instances automated behavior is the preferred mental process—such as the reflex action in which you duck, dodge, swerve, or pause without hesitation or conscious planning—and it may have saved your life. Conversely, that same process can result in a tragic outcome if you succumb to it in a moment of anger or important decision making. Unfortunately, without training, the brain's processes cannot distinguish when these conditioned, unconscious responses are effective or debilitating.

When the emotional limbic brain is triggered by the RAS, our cerebral cortex shuts down, and we begin operating in the instinctive fight-or-flight behavior mode. After the emotion subsides and we begin to relax, the RAS trigger switches us back into the more logical and creative cerebral cortex. This explains why losing control of your emotions in a situation can render you incapable of thinking clearly and responding intelligently. When dealing with stressful situations involving my teenagers, I seem to be able to constructively deal with whatever issue is confronting me if I can control my emotional responses. I can even speak coherently. When I lose my temper, however, I am reduced to such mindless platitudes as "Because I said so," or, "As long as you live in my house . . ." Because speech resides in the new, conscious brain, the RAS limits my working vocabulary when I am emotionally charged.

Unconscious Thought and Emotions

Your reactions are so ingrained in you that it is all too easy to become ignorant of the workings of your thoughts and emotions. Emphasis on activity, doing something all the time, keeps you more focused upon action rather than the experience. You lose touch with how you really feel, think, and sense. When this occurs, you lose your creative energy. You increasingly act and react like the rest of the tribe because you fail to observe your own internal wisdom.

Ignoring yourself makes you feel restless and unfulfilled. You do not know why you do not know what you want; you just know that what you are doing is not it. You seem to be tired all the time when you are not energized by frantic activity. Losing touch with yourself makes it increasingly easy to compartmentalize your life. You separate work, family, play, and spirit as if these were different file drawers in your internal file cabinet. You increase your focus upon getting things done, rather than how you are doing.

Emotions Color Our Behavior

"We are feeling beings before we are thinking beings," says William Grey, director of a psychiatric clinic in

Massachusetts. "Emotional nuances play a primary and organizing role in cognition," he says.[1] These emotions are imprinted upon your thoughts and ideas at the hidden limbic level of your brain's operation. The emotional response sets the pattern through which the thinking will be filtered. Responding to what it first notices, the brain is programmed to react in a predetermined pattern.

Author Richard Dawkins introduced his Darwinian concept of ideological struggle in the book, *The Selfish Gene*. People's emotions linked to their thoughts carry a good deal of influence regarding the survival or death of their ideas. These emotions have been responsible for more behavior than any other stimulus. Although some of our functioning has become more apparent to us as it has moved from our unconscious to conscious mind, our emotional responses can still be quite primitive, often manifesting strong feelings, attitudes, and even actions—while keeping the source of these feeling hidden from us. For example, an adult might have a strong aversion to strawberries because he was stung by bees as a young child while picking strawberries. He associates an emotion with strawberries, despite having no clear memory of the event.

Our thinking is formed out of our perception of an event filtered through our experiences. Hard as it is for some people to accept, all events are neutral. They simply are what they are. Events have no prejudice, opinions, preferences, or feelings. People do. But when people encounter events, they overlay them with attitudes and feelings. This point is where the mental interaction begins. People do not experience the event; rather, they experience their feelings regarding the event. Thoughts are born out of feelings, and the event is filtered through the individual's perspective.

[1] Gabriel Lusser Rico, *Writing the Natural Way* (New York: G.P. Putnam's Sons, 1983), page 17.

Emotional Anticipation of Events Colors Perception

"Worrying is creating," writes Dawna Markova, who once worked with a group of senior women with high blood pressure. "Every afternoon, they'd sit in the lobby of the nursing home, swapping stories about whose children were the most negligent, or whose grandchildren were most likely to end up dead in a drug war, and which of them was next to be delegated to the charity wards for the terminally ill." Dr. Markova goes on to say she asked a nurse to monitor the blood pressure after these sessions and discovered, medication or not, the group's blood pressure was higher after the complaining. Dr. Markova worked with the group and taught them the art of constructive worrying, teaching them to transform worries from "soap operas to success stories." She reports, "The nurse called me the next week and reported a remarkable drop in the blood pressure levels of every woman in the group."[2]

Emotionally reacting to or emotionally anticipating an event of which you have insufficient information to take action is an exercise in futility. Have you ever rehearsed a conversation in anticipation of a confrontation that never happened? Or if the confrontation did happen, it did not occur in the way you anticipated? Emotional rehearsing or anticipating, we soon realize, is a wasted effort. It is allowing our emotions about an event to interfere with our thinking at the deeper, creative mind level. As discussed earlier, by anticipating the negative, we often attract it.

---

[2] Excerpted from *No Enemies Within* by Dawna Markova, Copyright 1994 Dawna Markova, by permission from Conari Press.

Process

Imagine that you are seated in the dark. You can see nothing. All around you are noises and motions that you are aware of but cannot see. You are unable to define what these things are. You feel alone, and the things that are happening around you are fearful.

Slowly the light level seems to rise. Now you are able to make out the outlines of things passing in a misty state around you. They seem to come out of nowhere until they are near and then they fade into the mist. The outlines look like masks of various types and designs. As the light level gets stronger and brighter, you begin to make out the faces on the masks. You understand they are emotions: fear, envy, jealousy, and anger. Slowly you begin to perceive other people in the misty distance. Your fear starts falling away as you realize that nothing here can really hurt you, only scare you.

The light continues to get brighter and brighter as you continue to see more clearly. The surroundings begin to take on a somewhat macabre, fun-house nature. The light continues to increase until it is brilliant. You notice that you are holding something in your hand. Suddenly you realize that it is the light level control. You have been controlling the light level all along.

With this realization, a new level of understanding floods over you. Your calm becomes deeper, and your earlier fears and discomfort fall away. You realize everything has been an illusion. The space becomes brighter still. You know you did not turn up your light level. You suddenly realize that the others around you have turned up theirs. You see that everyone has their own remote control. Each remote only adjusts the individual's light, but as others increase their lights, the overall light level is also increased. At that moment you understand the difference between controlling your perceptions and controlling the events around you. You realize that the events are outside of your control, yet in understanding this, the events seem to become more controllable and less threatening.

This is the process of awakening. A mystic might call it enlightenment. It is not some obscure mystical practice from another time and place. It is simply "up-leveling" your awareness and perceptions regarding what is going on around you and how you are interacting to co-create your experience of it. After learning to separate how you feel from what is occurring, you begin to sense and think differently.

Isolate Events From Feelings

Isolating events from your feelings about events is necessary for a fully functioning transformation. It not only changes how you think about those things you did not know, but it also redefines those things you thought you previously understood. Events or conditions themselves do not change, yet the possibilities available to you do change when this awareness occurs.

The creative mind seeks to get behind the feelings we have surrounding an event to recreate our attitudes and actions in more positive and useful ways. Uncovering your unconscious reasoning releases your creative expression. It frees you from your hypnosis. Awakening, you see the true composition of your thinking. When you see the reasoning behind your thinking, because you have isolated the feelings, you can consciously choose to redirect your thinking in new ways—ways that result in a more positive experience for yourself.

Although you cannot always control the outcomes in situations, you can control your feelings about the outcomes. Allowing emotion to undermine your creativity, you become locked into a perception that is masking the reality of creative possibilities. When you are reacting to the event, at an emotional level, your focus is on the problem—not the opportunity. Your mind becomes mired in your emotional pit the longer your feelings' focus is activated. Events do not limit your choices; only your thinking about events. A great deal of emotion may be generated at the event level of situations, but little of it is useful for constructive change.

Prepare for Events Without Anticipating Them

It is possible to prepare for events without anticipating them. The trick to this level of openness and flexibility is maintaining a relaxed state and a receptive attitude. This approach enables you to see opportunities. Sometimes, however, your emotional reaction is both unconscious and happening faster than you can control. Keeping open and aware requires that we practice the state of being mindful.

Mindfulness Training

Our thoughts and attitudes about events fuel our actions. The "what you do" is a result of how you respond. Practicing separating the feeling from the event is the focus of mindfulness training. Mindful practices awaken your creative mind by revealing the errors, illusions, and false assumptions in your thinking. Mind-fulness directs the creative mind to go behind the reactive mind.

Mindful being is simply bringing your direct aware-ness into some simple activity or process. Doing so relaxes you and simultaneously stimulates your unconscious, cre-ative mind to recreate patterns without interruption. Many activities can be thought of as mindful. Some meditative forms are referred to as mindful. An example of mindful meditation is focusing your mind on your breathing, not allowing distractions to unsettle your mind, and moving it away from your focus on the breath. Mindfulness may also be thought of as awareness. Simply becoming fully aware of the moment in which we are participating is a mindful act. Becoming fully aware of eating, walking, shaving, and washing the dishes are all simple examples of mindfulness.

Morita

In a Japanese form of psychotherapy called Morita, the feelings, thoughts, and actions are separated so the indi-vidual can understand and bring control to his or her life. In Morita, it is understood that someone might have a feeling or sensation that might cause him or her to wish to strike another in anger. Acting upon that feeling would not be considered an acceptable response. Morita acknowledges the feeling but does not allow for the acting out that might accompany it. For this reason, an insanity plea would not be an acceptable excuse for misbehavior.

Practice Exercise

Mindfulness

Make a list of hobbies and activities that you enjoy that might be considered mindful. Choose one or two of these activities to spend time doing on a regular basis, about 30 minutes to one hour three times a week. Enjoy the little rewards of your focused attention. Slow down your pace when practicing these mindful activities. When involved in mindful activities, always remember to practice slow, rhythmic breathing. If you discover yourself becoming anxious or agitated by any event, bring your awareness back to the breathing and observe breathing for five to seven breaths. Do not allow yourself to become rushed or hurried. If thoughts relating to things other than what you are doing rise in the mind, simply let them pass with the moment. Allow your whole self to be occupied in the moment. Upon completing this exercise each day, see how long you can continue the slower, more mindful pace as you focus on other areas of your life.

Journal Practice

Isolate Emotions

Write down all the places where you seem to become most stressed, inflexible, and out of balance. In each instance, attempt to identify the circumstance, individuals, and feelings that are involved in the event. After you have generated a number of examples, begin isolating each of the three characteristics: circumstance, individuals, and feelings, and begin seeking common and recurring patterns within them. For example, you might note under circumstances that you have a high number of entries that occur early in the morning when you first get to work, or right after work when you arrive home. By observing this pattern, you may notice that both circumstances follow your commute each day. Does driving at rush hour cause stress for you? Do the feelings you have when commuting in rush-hour traffic seem to correspond with any other stress-induced feelings? Can you change that condition of commuting in rush hour by either going to work earlier, later, or telecommuting some days? If you cannot change the condition, what can you do to change your feelings about it?

Many insights will occur to you as you begin to keep a journal of activities on a regular basis. Over time, patterns of thoughts, feelings, and behavior will become increasingly obvious to you. Often, change can occur quickly and easily once you've first taken time to see the condition and your pattern of responding to it.

6

We don't all learn
the same way.

"Whatever interests, is interesting."
—William Hazlitt

Principle

Most of us find that learning comes more easily when
the information is communicated in a specific manner.
Some people process information visually, some audibly,
and some kinesthetically. See it, hear it, or do it—the
impact of those simple observations is more profound
than we might realize. Our learning style, like our preferred intelligences, influences what information we
understand and emphasize in processing our experiences. Many of us do not appreciate why we sometimes
cannot seem to comprehend information, while other
times it comes so easily to us. Many teachers are equally
unaware of learning styles or fail to understand their
importance. These three aspects of communication and

learning styles, visual, auditory, and kinesthetic—can be seen in "What is Your Communication Style?"

Visual-Dominant Learners

Visual-dominant learners comprehend through visual stimulation. These individuals like to see the information they are learning. From pictures and motion to colors and reading, they enjoy and learn best when their vision is engaged in the learning process. If you are a visual learner, stimulate yourself with a variety of visual devices—graphs, pictures, slides, charts, and overheads in bright colors. These pictorials containing all the information to be learned will heighten the learning process and will accelerate and increase your retention. Visual learners emphasize what is seen, rather than what is heard. Sometimes visual learners "do not see your point," "cannot believe their eyes," or "see eye-to-eye with you."

Auditory-Dominant Learners

Auditory-dominant learners enjoy the rapport of communication with one another and feel most intellectually engaged when in a conversation or dialogue with other people. Auditory learners would just as soon hear a tape as read a book. When the speaker is interesting, they can learn well in a lecture environment. Auditory learners "tell it like it is" and "can turn a deaf ear when they tune you out," unless it "sounds good to them."

When visuals are combined with auditory information, the auditory learner will primarily retain what is heard, and the visual learner will primarily retain what is seen. If you are an auditory learner, discussing and hearing the information will most effectively accelerate your learning. Music can also be highly effective in stimulating you when working on projects or learning new information.

What Is Your Communication Style?

Visual

See what I mean
Get the picture
Are clear on the issue
Have the perspective
Visualize the result
Can be foggy on the details
Show you results

Auditory

Hears what you are saying
Sounds you out on an idea
Wants to be in tune with the group
Likes to discuss the details
Does not want to be off-key
Likes harmony

Kinesthetic

Feels the pressure
Likes a hands-on approach
Can get out of synchronization
Wants to be in touch with you
Senses the "vibes"
Can be clumsy on the details

Kinesthetic-Dominant Learners

Kinesthetic-dominant learners are physical learners who learn more from acting and moving than from reading and viewing. Kinesthetic individuals require more hands-on opportunities and learn more from engaging in exercises and activities. These learners "dance to a different drummer" and "know when it does not feel right," so "lay all your cards on the table" with kinesthetic learners.

Kinesthetic learners require less visual and verbal information and more opportunities to practice and participate in the skills, process, or information being presented. For them, learning is less intellectual and more experiential. If you are a kinesthetic learner, look for ways to engage your participation in the learning process with "Hands-on" types of instruction. You can accelerate your learning best by actively participating and practicing the new information.

The Evolution of Learning Styles

Human learning has adapted to meet our environment. Once, we primarily learned by watching and imitating with our physical action. Physical dexterity played a much more critical role in our ancestors' survival than in our lives today. As language developed, emphasis on words and symbols became greater—hence auditory and later visual learning.

Increasingly, with the explosion of visual media such as television and computers, new generations of learners are inheriting stronger visual dominance in their learning preferences. Research has shown that children can process visual information as much as four times faster than previous generations as a result of their increased exposure to these visual influences.

Process

As a self-directed learner, it is important for you to understand your preferred communication style so that when you choose to acquire new information, learn some new skill, or improve your performance, you choose learning techniques that play up to your favored communication process. Failing to learn is often a result of failing to engage your style in acquiring the new information. Try taking the "Communication Styles Preference Test" later in this chapter to determine your favored learning style.

Use Your Preferred Style to Learn New Information

If you are an auditory learner, consider the tape over the book. Learn French from a French-speaking individual with whom you can spend an hour or two twice a week talking. Visual learners might prefer the French book, as well as other visual devices, such as posters with key words and phrases, mounted upon the wall, to maximize their learning. Kinesthetic learners will learn more in role-playing situations, like creating a French meal with an instructor, visiting a museum, or working with an interactive instruction game.

When you have learned your favored style, you will find an abundance of information about how to increase your learning effectiveness.

Try Using Other Learning Styles

Secondly, and equally important, is learning to appreciate and use styles other than your preferred style. Learning to use a less familiar communication style can be difficult at first. The process may initially seem awkward or counter-intuitive when you first attempt learning in this manner. Working within a non-dominant area, however, will often produce profound discoveries in both what we learn and how we learn by effectively cross-training our brain. Discovering which learning styles are most suited to what type of content can provide you with guidance when looking for cross-training opportunities.

When I first began studying T'ai Chi, it seemed counter-intuitive. Moving my body and balancing myself was difficult to the point of seeming impossible at times. Although I had to work twice as hard as many students to whom the movements came more easily, several of them dropped out of the class more quickly. Perhaps they were not challenged. Or perhaps, when the form became too challenging, they dropped out because they were not used to encountering difficulty in an intelligence style in which they normally felt comfortable. For whatever reason, learning kinesthetically took me longer, yet looking back on the expereience, I feel I learned more than just the T'ai Chi form.

I refused to quit. Buoyed by little successes and a supportive teacher, I became known as the water buffalo in the herd of gazelles. In spite of the difficulty, I stayed. Eventually all the others who had begun before me had dropped out of the program. Perseverance became my best instructor as I became more comfortable with my body's kinesthetic intelligence.

As I began teaching at the encouragement of my instructor, I saw others discovering what I had learned about the T'ai Chi form and how awkward it felt in the beginning. The form asked students to move in ways they did not have experience moving. They could not access the kinesthetic mind with their logical, verbal, or interpersonal skills. Ultimately, it was the interpersonal, kinesthetic experience that taught them what they needed to learn to begin to understand the form.

Students who have continued to practice, many of whom were not at first naturals, have learned many of the same lessons. What once seemed impossibly frustrating has now become totally intuitive. What was once awkward is now graceful. What once our bodies could not see, we now see easily. What we have learned from the practice, we apply every day in how we process our world and move through life.

People transfer the wisdom of new learning, and the process of how they learn, into every other area of their body of knowledge. Through cross-training, you create a crossover effect that results in a profound impact upon multiple aspects of your thinking and being. It is as if when we change one aspect of our thinking, it correspondingly changes all other aspects of our lives to include this new discovery and corresponding intelligence.

I have one student who came to T'ai Chi with enormous limitations. When she first began T'ai Chi study, she could not walk comfortably swinging her arms in a rhythmic manner. She also did not have the balance to stand on one leg. She recounted, as I began to get to know her, being tall and thin as a child with slowly developing motor skills. Her awkwardness was ridiculed by her family and friends, resulting in her "becoming painfully shy and reserved" throughout her life. She complained of constant back and neck discomfort and was nervous and tense most of the time. She was 66 when she decided to learn T'ai Chi.

One year later, she laughs spontaneously as she tells some of the new students how she felt when she began. Her back and neck pain is now mostly a memory. She moves with much more grace and balance and walks naturally and comfortably. Equally dramatic is her change in disposition and attitude. This once-reserved and shy student now often helps newcomers relax with her wit and humor. Recently she proudly showed me her bowling scores, which had greatly improved over last season. I asked her if she felt T'ai Chi had been influential in improving the scores. "Well," she responded, "I don't bounce the ball down the alley any more." T'ai Chi had clearly produced cross-training results for this woman.

Communication Styles Preference Test

Take this simple test to determine your preferred style. Respond with a yes or no to each group of 10 questions. Do not spend too much time thinking about your answers; rather, trust your first impressions.

Part I

____ 1. Do you prefer face-to-face meetings over telephone meetings?

____ 2. Do you enjoy reading magazines with lots of pictures?

____ 3. Would you rather attend a play than go dancing?

____ 4. Do people say you sometimes speak too quickly?

____ 5. Do you enjoy the planning and organizing process?

____ 6. Do you doodle when speaking on the phone or thinking?

____ 7. When spelling, do you see the word in your mind?

____ 8. Do you usually notice changes in others' personal appearances?

____ 9. Would you rather read a story than have a story read to you?

____10. When you breathe, do you notice it most in the upper chest?

Part II

____11. Are noises sometimes distracting to you when you are working?

____12. Can you remember the melody to a favorite song more easily than the words?

____13. Would you prefer a telephone call to a face-to-face meeting?

____14. Would you rather hear a concert than go to an art show?

____15. Do you frequently talk to yourself when working?

____16. When spelling, do you often sound out the words in your mind?

____17. When breathing, do you feel the breath evenly in your chest?

___18. Do you find long, intense conversations enjoyable?

___19. Do you find yourself stirred by a good public speaker?

___20. Would you rather hear a story than read a story?

Part III

___21. Do you enjoy exercises and activities more than books or lectures when learning?

___22. Would you rather go dancing than listen to a band?

___23. When you spell, do you often write down the word?

___24. Would coworkers say you "think well on your feet?"

___25. Do you prefer reading action stories over stories with dialogue and description?

___26. Are you good at jigsaw puzzles?

___27. Do you frequently gesture when speaking?

___28. Is it difficult for you to sit still?

___29. Do you frequently touch others when speaking to them?

___30. Do you notice your breathing most in your lower chest or stomach?

Scoring:

Total the number of yes answers in each part. If you had more yes responses in Part I, you prefer visual communication; more yes answers in Part II means you prefer auditory communication; and more yes answers in Part III means you are a kinesthetic communicator. Your intensity of preference will be indicated by the number of yes responses in each category. A high yes or no count in one category may indicate a stronger degree of preference.

Our minds gather and retain information in a variety of ways.

"What we nurture in ourselves we grow; that's nature's eternal law."
—Goethe

Principle

Our minds are constantly gathering information in one of four ways—intellectually, emotionally, physically, or intuitively. Too many of us are, unfortunately, unaware of how powerfully informative the latter three of these informational gathering resources are. Because so many people are out of touch with their feelings and physical bodies, they often fail to perceive these information processes and signals—and, as a result, are suspicious or fail to comprehend and respond when these informative signals are sent.

Over-emphasis on logic develops the intellectual mind without regard to how this imbalance undermines and devalues your other information-gathering systems.

Logic is most useful in evaluating alternatives in the creative process. Gathering those alternatives is the role of your other informative systems—supporting the more generative aspects of your mind. These information-gathering senses of feelings, body, and intuition reveal information and alternatives not available in any other way.

The Emotional Mind

The emotional mind is not confined to the space above your ears. Our feeling mind is constantly involved in everything we do and think about. That you are often not aware of its presence is more a result of your lack of awareness, than its lack of involvement in thinking. Using your entire system of self to gather feeling and awareness of sensations, the emotional union works at a sensory non-verbal and non-intellectual level.

Every decision you make is impacted by feelings. To be unaware of how those feelings are created and how they influence your choices is to be hypnotized to your true, totally functioning self. Bringing your awareness to them and sensing their role in influencing and shaping your understanding empowers your creative mind to utilize them productively, making you more fully functioning.

Although overly analytical skeptics might proclaim they are not emotionally involved in their work and only deal with factual information, I have found that they can become greatly emotional in their defense of their non-emotionality. I am most fearful of those whose feelings are so deeply hidden that they are unable to acknowledge and comprehend them, even while those feelings are blindly driving them.

The Physical Mind

Pick up a pencil or pen and write a sentence. Do you feel the friction of the surface as the point slides across the page? Where do you feel the feeling: at the point of the writing instrument, or in your fingers? Maybe you feel it in your mind? The illusion of that place where we make contact is our intellect attempting to define a sensory occurrence. Sensory information, such as feelings and physical information, occur through our entire being. Information is constantly moving both from the cell to the brain and from the brain to the cell.

Physical learning is utilizing the cellular memory and mind to drive our learning. Although you can analyze and diagram the movements of a ballet performer in minute detail and precision, you can never know the movement without actually experiencing it. You cannot experience it mentally or intellectually—only through the physical experience of your body.

Our physical minds are far removed from our intellectual minds in the experience of movement and practice. Our limbic and reptilian brains are more involved in our comprehension and memory of each action. We do not remember with words; we remember with sensations.

The enormity of these differences became most obvious to me the first time I attempted to find words to express T'ai Chi movement while I was doing it. My verbal, logical mind was befuddled, and my cerebral cortex was speechless. Because these aspects of mind were little involved in my physical learning, I had no language to express the movement. I had to struggle to discover and create a language that explained what I wanted students to do. My mind was as unformed as the beginners' minds.

The Intuitive Mind

Intuition is information gained outside the normal senses. This level of awareness requires practice in experiencing subtle states of information and recognition of nuance energies. Intuition combines the body mind, logical mind, and emotional mind in its operation. You might consider it thinking with the gut, which may in reality be a more accurate explanation of what is occurring, because your stomach contains a great number of neural receptors—second only to your brain.

Your intuitive mind, or sixth sense, provides you information through the parallel processing right hemisphere. While your left hemisphere processes information that you perceive as logical, five-sensory, and verbal, the right hemisphere is processing the world in a completely different manner. Neuro-scientific discoveries have now given us the capacity to know how we might come to understand this form of information. Through research, the systems that process these parallel and unfamiliar signals are becoming more observable and hopefully more familiar to us.

A clear indication that this process is occurring is revealed through hypnosis. When hypnotized, people who have been under anesthetic during an operation frequently recall specific details of the operation that occurred while they were seemingly "out." Numerous experiments have demonstrated this extrasensory system's ability to provide information to individuals who were asleep, unconscious, or anesthetized.

Because you and I are unable to recognize, think about, or verbalize this extrasensory information, we often resist it or remain unaware of it. Many people distrust or resist understanding this information-gathering system because of their over-dependence on their logical, reasoning mind.

Sometimes your gut feeling, vibes, or intuition are your most reliable assets in an unfamiliar situation. This nonlogical process operating beneath our conscious logical mental level can influence us dramatically when we learn to sense and understand it. It is most often perceived as a sense of knowing without knowing how you know. It arrives unexpectedly and with a sense of certainty.

I have asked thousands of seminar attendees, "When your logic and your intuition disagree, which one is the most reliable source of information and guidance?" Almost universally they agree: intuition. If, however, I ask them to explain it, they struggle. Your verbal skills are logical, left-hemisphered. Intuition is non-verbal, instinctive intelligence that does not have any words to express itself. Instinct may, in fact, emanate from our body and feelings sensing the vibrational energy that permeates the space around us.

Many highly effective people utilize intuition, although they may be reluctant to volunteer its contribution to their decision process. Too often individuals at a loss to explain how intuition works are reluctant to give credence or voice to its insights. Gut instinct, funny feelings, or a sixth-sense are all expressions we use to describe this method of knowing that Joel Barker, author of *Paradigm Principles*, calls one of the primary tools of making the paradigm shift.

The Intelligence Myth

Let's face it. Some people seem to be more successful at gathering, processing, and retaining information than others. We are all aware of the *Intelligence Quotient* (IQ) test. It was initially developed by French psychologist Alfred Binet at the turn of the century to identify school children in need of remedial help. It was later expanded and modified by Stanford psychologist Lewis Terman. Terman, who created the idea of an intelligence quotient measurement system, believed the test would help educators to identify those individuals whose mental abilities should prohibit them from spreading their genes into the gene pool. His ideas were not inconsistent with the then prevailing scientific communities' emphasis on nature over nurture as the precondition for success and achievement.

Here is the fallacy: There is more to brain power than can be measured on a single IQ test. The single intelligence theory can measure an individual's ability to generate one answer to eight specific types of question groupings: the ability to follow instructions, abstract ability, speed in responding, vocabulary recognition, reading skills, verbal reasoning, math skills, and numerical reasoning. At best, a single IQ measurement tests your ability to do the specific type of thinking the test is measuring at the time the test is taken. These tests have no provision for your ability to go beyond the stated problem with your answer. The test is not a useful tool in predicting your ability in making decisions in complex situations, or measuring your human relations capacity, your creativity, or even your ability to succeed at the game of life.

New theories of intelligence have come a long way in helping us understand more about the nature of how we learn and how we can continue to learn. Unlike the old single intelligence theory that assumed we never got smarter than the single test measured, these new approaches demonstrate how we actually can get smarter with age and how the intelligence we might call wisdom helps us improve our mental functioning over time.

Various models for intelligence development have been conceived, but nearly all models now show that intelligence is more than a single trait that can be measured by an individual test of a few hours. Different intelligences can simultaneously be learning from different aspects of the information available.

Gardner's Eight Intelligences

Howard Gardner, a Harvard psychologist and educator, has identified and developed over the past few years a theory constructed around eight human intelligences. Although criticized by some single intelligence proponents, Gardner's logic is founded on several reasonable observations, including: each intelligence category involves specific cognitive operations; each intelligence category can be isolated in such a manner that brain injury can eradicate it; and finally, genius performance can be specifically demonstrated in each of the areas.

Here is a brief description of Gardner's eight intelligence categories.

1. Logical: Think sequential, analytical, and abstract. This intelligence is capable of long chains of reasoning useful in mathematics, the sciences, and even detective work.

2. Linguistic: Emphasizes itself through word choice, rhetoric, and meaning. Writers and speakers utilize this intelligence when they communicate with language.

3. Musical: This concept is the intelligence of understanding the complex nature of sounds. Pitches, rhythms, and vibrational levels are all isolated and categorized with this intelligence. Professions as diverse as musicians and auto mechanics can value this intelligence.

4. Intrapersonal: This self-reflective intelligence enables us to define and set goals for performance based upon our previous efforts. Insight into feelings and distinguishing the impact of such things as mood and behavior are part of this intelligence. Psychologists and researchers share this skill.

5. Interpersonal: Interpersonal is the ability to relate and understand others and communicate effectively with them. Teachers and effective leaders use this intelligence to send and receive information with their audiences.

6. Spatial: Image perception, transformation, and recreating graphic images are elements of this intelligence, including an eye for symmetry and balance and the ability to look at two-dimensional renderings and see the three-dimensional product. Spatial vision is a trait shared by artists and designers.

7. Kinesthetic: Kinesthetic is the intelligence of physical movement. From people who are good with their hands to athletes, this agility intelligence enables individuals to learn through movement of their bodies. This intelligence is as important to a surgeon as it is to a quarterback.

8. Naturalist: This concept is a relatively new addition to the model. It focuses upon the intelligence of classifying, understanding, and utilizing features of the environment. The ability to develop a rapport with animals and nature are characteristic of the naturalist intelligence.

Most people tend to favor a limited number of intelligences clustered around categories. What we often consider genius is a highly developed capacity in one area of intelligence. High development in one area at the expense of another might explain why we sometimes refer to some individuals as "nerds" or "eggheads."

High scoring in one area seldom has any correlation to equal abilities in other areas. In fact, multiple high tendencies are rare. Prodigal performance in one area can even result in what might be considered as idiot savant tendencies and would be considered disfunctionality in other areas. The norm seems to be two or three areas of above-average competence, one or two average, and the remainder below-average.

Observing people's abilities through these eight different intelligences, you quickly come to understand how certain individuals can score so poorly on single intelligence tests and yet become so effective and successful in the real world. Most people favor those areas in which they discover an aptitude. Successful people are generally those individuals whose personal and professional lives are built upon those intelligences they favor.

Process

As the intellect, emotional, physical, and intuitive processes become more fully awakened, they release the creative mind of your higher potential. We are all capable of multiple minds, or levels of consciousness, and the formative creative mind is your highest level of consciousness. It is the mind that comes to understand the co-creational ability we all possess that allows us to more actively participate and influences the quality of our lives.

Self-Actualization: Developing the Four Minds

Sleeping is a low level of mental consciousness. In the sleeping state, our minds are not inactive—but rather cycle through various patterns that include deep sleep, REM states (rapid eye movement), and dream states. The ordinary, wakeful state consciousness is that state that most of us identify as being ourselves. In this state, we believe we have a full awareness of what is going on around us, as well as a sense of ourselves. This level of mental activity, however, is the level that is automated and hypnotized to both itself and the higher states.

Highly focused states of consciousness occur when some aspect of mind causes us to isolate our focus on some event or feeling. Here, we are aware of our hypnosis because (sometimes only after the event) we become unaware of other external activities. Completely lost in our absorption, we become totally sensory-connected in something. Becoming emotionally distraught in a crisis is as much an example of this altered mental state as totally focusing on sharpening a knife.

At the transcendent mental state, we become aware of more subtle levels of internal and external energy. In transcendent states, we can sense the energy of a group of people in a room or the calm energy of nature in the deep forest—even the mental action of another. At this state, we are not yet able to interact and use the energy constructively and for our own and others' well-being.

At the highest transcendent state, we are open to and aware of a vibrational level of activity that reveals our total connectedness to everything around us. In this state, some people see auras; others perceive thoughts or physical and mental conditions. At this level, we become co-creational with the energies around us working with both the knowledge and wisdom that is revealed to us. Once the transcendent mind is awakened in this way, the experience is never forgotten.

Because the creative formative mind is fully conscious, it is not hypnotized to its actions. It not only sees existing patterns but is able to form new patterns easily because it is not habitually committed to responding in limiting ways. This idea is the mind the Zen practitioner refers to as "big mind." This mind is the source of your unlimited creative potential—whole brain involvement in your full functionality. Using all these ways of learning elevates your mind to what psychologist Abraham Maslow would call self-actualization. When our creative mind is awakened, we begin to see all the possibilities of the beginner.

Emotional Mind

Developing a feeling awareness requires tuning out external distractions and bringing the mind into the feeling body. Because feelings are predominately associated with the right hemisphere activity and limbic brain, you cannot develop an understanding of them through emphasis on verbal or intellectual practices. Feelings, like physical learning, must be experienced through direct contact of awareness and experience. Rather than thinking brain, one must think heart. Bringing the mind into one's heart can reveal emotional awareness and understanding.

Physical Mind

Opening the physical mind means moving your sense of self out of the head and into the body. Physical learning comes through repetition, experience, and practice. In T'ai Chi, we discover that little leaps of ability occur almost magically when we repeat movement, follow a proper form, and observe ourselves to remember what we are doing. Eventually, the physical mind begins learning these movements without the use of logical processes.

Intuitive Mind

Intuition will never communicate with you in a manner that fits normal methods of understanding, so it is necessary when seeking these messages to engage in some activities that facilitate their release. Use dance, movement, music, meditation, visualization, dream awareness, mindful practices, or other right hemisphere-stimulating exercises. Intuition will arrive as feelings, visual images, or symbols, or sudden unexplainable senses or mood shifts—even in your dreams. Sometimes simply asking your intuitive self for help and being open to the possibility of insight is all that is required to access the support of the intuitive mind. These insights, when they arrive, are not difficult to recognize. Immediately writing down one's dreams when arising in the morning can be insightful to intuition, awareness, and understanding.

Three important considerations exist in understanding your intuition, and used together, they can help you separate garbage from guidance. First, intuition is not logical, so messages will often be provided in symbolic or non-logical ways. Second, intuition is holistic—big picture all-at-once experiences—which means that you will get most insights in a complete or finished form. What you will not get is a linear pattern of, "This will happen, then this will happen, and so on." Intuition rarely works in a sequential way. Finally, intuition is a non-emotional system. When messages initially arrive, they will do so in calm, detached ways that do not betray any feelings. If feelings are accompanying your sense, then it is either not intuition, or you are putting emotion on top of the message you have received.

Intuition is not infallible. Often what we perceive as intuition is completely wrong. Sometimes we misinterpret the information. Like any decision-making process, you are never going to be 100 percent accurate. Combining your non-logical knowing with your logical analytical processes can, however, increase your rate of accuracy. It is not difficult to humor your hunches by evaluating your intuitive messages using logical left-side critical thinking and investigation. Sometimes further discovery, research, or inquiry provides insightful validation for those funny little feelings you had about an idea.

Cross-Training Intelligence Preferences

When you continue to develop your abilities in specific modalities, you increase your overall performance in other modalities. While improvement in a dominant intelligence area can boost your ability and performance in that area, improvement in a lower ability modality can boost your performance across the entire spectrum of intelligences.

Tony Buzan, author of *Using Both Sides of Your Brain*, writes, "Subsequent research showed that when people were encouraged to develop a mental area they had previously considered weak, this development, rather than detracting from other areas, seemed to produce synergistic effect in which all areas of mental performance improved."[1]

Piano keyboard instruction has been shown to significantly increase spatial temporal reasoning in preschoolers. Exposure to certain musical rhythms has been shown to so positively affect spatial reasoning that Georgia Governor Zell Miller, in 1997, proposed that the state legislature introduce legislation to make available brain-enhancing music to parents of newborns in the state.

Educator Elaine De Beauport has demonstrated remarkable results by teaching math and English students art, dancing, and storytelling. Students in her program show dramatic improvement in working at their peak abilities as a result of this cross-training process. "Children who were flunking math were helped to visualize equations. After taking art courses, they could access numbers through images," De Beauport wrote. De Beauport effectively did away with 'learning disabilities' at her school and helped every student work at the top of his or her ability.[2]

This cross-training effect has also been observed in developing artistic expression. Painters report improved visual expression as a result of intensive writing exercises, and writers report writing breakthroughs when exploring their visual intelligence through workshops and instruction. This "creative connection," as it is called by psychologist Natalie Rogers, is a foundational aspect of cross-training.

---

[1] Tony Buzan, *Using Both Sides of Your Brain* (New York: Penguin Group, 1991), page 17.

[2] Valerie Andrews, "The Three Faces of Mind," *Intuition*, Issue 19, December 1997, pages 26–27.

Spatial and kinesthetic activities seem to accentuate crossover benefits by moving the thinking processes out of the most frequently used areas of the brain and into areas less utilized. Frequently, this move shifts our thinking into the physical, intuitive, and/or emotional minds that most people least utilize.

Finding new ways to increase your mental and creative performance is the goal of cross-training. Use the following Multiple Intelligence Test to determine where your strengths and opportunities lie. By using testing as a diagnostic device to prescribe cross-training learning opportunities, rather than as a measurement of your limitations, you can reinvent your concept of intelligence and begin improving your full functionality.

The Multiple Intelligence Quiz[3]

Which of the intelligences do you favor? What are your strengths? By answering the following questions, you will be able to gauge which forms of intelligence are your strongest and your weakest. This test will enable you to focus on making sure that you make the most of your existing abilities—and see whether you can develop some of the others.

Most of us have a mixed portfolio of intelligences, and there is no purpose in trying to simply label yourself as a "logical-mathematical" type or a "body-kinesthetic" type. The checklist is designed to help you develop a fuller appreciation of the intelligences you enjoy.

Give yourself one point for each statement that applies to you and tally each area for your total. Compare the overall totals from all eight intelligences, and you will readily see your greatest strengths and weaknesses. The higher your score, the more you favor that particular intelligence.

---

[3] From *Accelerated Learning* by Colin Rose. Copyright 1987 by Colin Rose. Used by permission of Dell Books, a division of Bantam Doubleday Dell Publishing Group, Inc.

Linguistic

1. You enjoy word play—making puns, tongue-twisters, and limericks. You enjoy poems, stories, and rhymes.

2. You read everything—books, magazines, newspapers, even product labels.

3. You can easily and confidently express yourself either orally or in writing; i.e., you are a persuasive debater and a good storyteller or writer.

4. You pepper your conversation with frequent allusions to things you have read or heard.

5. You like to do crosswords, play word games such as Scrabble®, or have a go at other word puzzles. You can spell well.

6. You have such an excellent vocabulary that people sometimes have to ask you to explain a word you have used. You enjoy using the precise word in context.

7. In school, you preferred subjects such as English, (language and literature) history, and social studies. You are conscious of the need to build your child's vocabulary.

8. You can hold your own in verbal arguments or debates, and you give clear directions and explanations.

9. You like to "think aloud," to talk through problems, to explain solutions, and to ask questions.

10. You can readily absorb information by listening to the radio or audio cassettes or lectures. The words are easily imprinted on your mind.

Total _____

Logical-Mathematical

1. You enjoy working with numbers and can do mental calculations.

2. You are interested in new scientific advances and like to experiment with things to see how they work.

3. You can easily balance your checkbook and do the household budget. You create numerical targets in your business and private life.

4. You like to put together a detailed itinerary for vacations or business trips. You often prepare, number, and implement a to-do list.

5. You enjoy the challenge of brainteasers or other puzzles and games that require logical and statistical thinking, e.g., checkers or chess.

6. You tend to readily identify the logical flaws in things people say and do.

7. Math and science were among your favorite subjects in school.

8. You can find specific examples to support a general point of view and feel comfortable analyzing situations and arguments.

9. You take a systematic, step-by-step approach to problem solving. You like to find patterns and relationships between objects or numbers.

10. You need to categorize, group, or quantify things to properly appreciate their relevance.

Total _____

Visual-Spatial

1. You have an appreciation of the visual arts and enjoy painting and sculpture. You have a good color sense.

2. You tend to make a visual record of events with a camera or camcorder.

3. You find yourself doodling when taking notes or thinking through something. You can draw quite accurately.

4. You have no problem reading maps and navigating. You have a good sense of direction.

5. You enjoy games such as jigsaw puzzles and mazes.

6. You are quite adept at taking things apart and putting them back together. You can assemble kits quite easily and can follow directions to do so.

7. In school, you liked lessons in art and preferred geometry to algebra.

8. You often make your point by providing a diagram or drawing and can interpret charts easily.

9. You can visualize how things look from a different perspective or how a building might look from a plan.

10. You prefer reading material that is heavily illustrated.

Total _____

Body-Kinesthetic

1. You take part in a sport or regularly perform some kind of physical exercise. You enjoy walks, swimming, and the sensation of using your body.

2. You are quite adept at "do-it-yourself" projects.

3. You like to think through problems while engaging in a physical pursuit, such as walking or running.

4. You do not mind getting up on the dance floor.

5. You like the most thrilling, body-contorting rides at the fun fair.

6. You need to physically handle something, to grasp it and manipulate it, to fully understand it. You enjoy jigsaws and model-making.

7. The most enjoyable classes in school were sports, physical education, and any handicrafts lessons. You enjoy sculpture as an art form.

8. You use hand gestures or other kinds of body language to express yourself.

9. You like rough-and-tumble play with children.

10. You need to tackle a new learning experience "hands on," rather than by reading a manual or watching a video.

Total _____

Musical

1. You can play a musical instrument.

2. You can manage to sing on key.

3. Usually you can remember a tune after hearing it just a couple of times.

4. You often listen to music at home and in your car, and you sometimes go to concerts. You like—even need—a musical background when you are working.

5. You find yourself tapping in time to music. You have a good sense of rhythm.

6. You can identify the sounds of different musical instruments.

7. Theme music or commercial jingles often pop into your head.

8. You cannot imagine life without music. You find that music easily evokes emotions and images for you as you listen to it.

9. You often whistle or hum a tune.

10. You often use rhythm (or rhyme) to remember things, e.g., saying a telephone number rhythmically.

Total _____

Interpersonal

1. You enjoy working with other people as part of a group or committee.

2. You take great pride in being a mentor or advisor to someone else.

3. People tend to come to you for advice. You could describe yourself as sympathetic.

4. You prefer team sports such as basketball, softball, soccer, and football to individual sports such as swimming and running.

5. You like games involving other people—bridge, Monopoly, and Trivial Pursuit.

6. You are a social butterfly. You would much prefer to be at a party than home alone watching television.

7. You have several very close, personal friends.

8. You communicate well with other people and can help resolve disputes.

9. You have no hesitation in taking the lead or showing the other people how to get things done.

10. You talk over problems with others, rather than trying to resolve them by yourself.

Total _____

Intrapersonal

1. You keep a personal diary or log to record your innermost thoughts.

2. You often spend "quiet time" reflecting on the important issues in your life.

3. You have set your own goals; you know where you are going.

4. You are an independent thinker; you know your own mind and make up your own mind.

5. You have a private hobby or interest that you do not really share with anyone else.

6. You like to go fishing by yourself or take a solitary hike. You are happy with your own company.

7. Your idea of a good vacation is an isolated hilltop cabin, rather than a five-star resort and lots of people.

8. You have a realistic idea of your own strengths and weaknesses.

9. You have attended self-improvement workshops or been through some kind of counseling to learn more about yourself.

10. You work for yourself or have seriously contemplated "doing your own thing."

Total _____

Naturalist

1. You keep or like pets.

2. You can recognize and name many different types of trees, flowers, and plants.

3. You have an interest in and a good knowledge of how the body works—where the main internal organs are, for example, and you keep abreast of health issues.

4. You are conscious of tracks, nests, and wildlife on a walk and can "read" weather signs.

5. You could envision yourself as a farmer, or maybe you like to fish.

6. You are a keen gardener and are familiar with the effects of the seasons.

7. You have an understanding of, and an interest in, the main global environmental issues.

8. You keep reasonably informed about the developments in astronomy, the origins of the universe, and the evolution of life.

9. You are interested in social issues, psychology, and human motivations.

10. You consider that conservation of resources and achieving sustainable growth are two of the biggest issues of our times.

Total _____

Practice Exercises

1. Physical Mind

In this next exercise, it is important that you first bring your breath all the way to the bottom of your lungs, approximately one inch below the navel. In bringing the breath down to this spot, you are also bringing your sense of self down to this spot. Moving, listening, and experiencing from this lower point awakens and encourages physical mindedness.

For this exercise, you will need a room with enough space to move about. You will also need a stereo that can play a cassette or CD and music that enables you to feel relaxed and peaceful. My suggestions for music include Vivaldi's "Four Seasons," Bach's cello suite, Chopin's "Emmanuel Acts in E Minor," Mozart's "Piano Con-certo No. 27," or perhaps something more New Age (Gabrielle Rote or David Darling)—you get the idea. Wear loose, comfortable clothing for this exercise. All movement in this exercise is done in slow motion, as if you were doing it underwater. As you become more comfortable with the movements, allow your body to experience the slow-motion movements in more and more detail.

Place your tongue at the palate against the back of the teeth at the roof of your mouth. Observing your inhalation through the nose, bring the breath into your body and down to the point one inch below the navel. See the air circulating around your lungs and imagine your stomach expanding and contracting with each intake of breath. Feel the energy of your body radiating outwardly from your center, touching all the things around you.

Begin the music. Standing with your legs shoulder-width apart, feet flat on the ground, imagine the weight of your body slowly sliding down from the top of your head toward your feet. Keeping your knees unlocked, slowly begin swaying with the music from side-to-side, hands hanging loosely, palms open, and fingers apart. Visualize yourself underwater, and the notes of the music are coming out of the speakers and floating into the space around you. Everything, including you, is moving in slow motion. Begin to sway your body like sea-grass in the currents, allowing your hands and arms to flow back and forth with your movement. Imagine you can gather the energy around you into your hand, scooping it up like water. Form it into a small ball using both hands. Shape the energy about the size of a bowling ball and hold it lightly in your hands. Note the feeling on your palms as you rotate the ball from side to side.

Notice the weight of the ball shifting in your palms as you pour it from one hand to the other. Make the ball of energy larger, feeling the weight increase. Become aware of the resistance of the space against your hands and arms as you continue to move in slow-motion. Once you begin feeling the weight of the ball and the resistance of the space, you can experiment with other movements in slow-motion, exploring the space and your senses as you move through it. See how slowly you can move and imagine you can feel the resistance of the space as your arms and legs move slowly through it.

Continue for as long as you like. Afterwards, sitting quietly, your mind unfocused, simply exploring and sensing the body. Often after this exercise, your body will experience a tingling sensation, and for a period afterward, your sense of physical self will be more acute.

2. Intuitive Mind

A. Anytime you wish to access your intuitive powers, begin by taking a deep breath and relaxing your entire body and mind. Once relaxed, bring your whole focus upon whatever you wish to gain information about. Do not force your mind, but rather allow your mind to simply enfold the area of interest. Using no mental force, simply hold the idea or object until you feel a sense of direction or information. Sometimes the information arrives shortly after you have released the mental focus. When this awareness occurs, it may be subtle, like a gentle nudging, or it may be instantaneous and insightful, but it is always simple and a completed thought that seems to come to you all at once.

B. Here are some non-threatening situations for intuitive practice:

→ Anytime you encounter a situation where you need to make a simple decision, ask yourself for intuitive guidance. For example, when seeking a parking place in a crowded lot, simply ask yourself, "Which aisle should I drive down?"

→ Anytime you encounter a line at a checkout, follow a hunch to choose which line will move faster.
→ Before entering a crowd or assembly of people, practice intuition by asking who you will encounter unexpectedly.

Journal Practice

Your Emotional Mind

Find a quiet place where you will not be interrupted and bring your journal. Do not analyze what you are doing; simply allow yourself to experience and record your feelings about it.

Sit in a comfortable position. Allow your arms and hands to lie loosely in your lap, your legs comfortable, feet flat on the floor. Close your eyes and bring your awareness to your breath. Place you tongue at the palate against the back of the teeth at the roof of your mouth. Observing your inhalation through the nose, bring the breath into your body and down to the center of your chest. See the air circulating around your heart and imagine your chest expanding and opening with each intake of breath. Feel the energy of your body radiating outwardly from your heart and touching all the things around you. Allow these radiated feelings to circulate back to you, bringing a feeling about what they encountered. Now bring your awareness into some situation where you would like to use your emotions to direct you. Using your heart awareness to "think" about that situation, ask yourself, how do I feel? What are my emotions about this? What are my true feelings? Do not dwell too much about the feelings and thoughts you experience; rather, simply be aware of them. Acknowledge and recognize them. Allow yourself to fully experience them. At the conclusion of this exercise, allow your awareness to come slowly back to your full self. Slowly open your eyes, without breaking the state you have created, and pick up your notebook and immediately begin writing down what you are feeling or did feel. Do not think about what you are writing, but simply let the words flow out of you and onto the page. Write as quickly as possibly, without going back to cross out or edit your words. Continue writing until you sense you have expressed all your feelings completely.

8

Complex movement stimulates complex thinking.

"There is guidance within each of us, and when we look and listen, we will hear the word."
—Ralph Waldo Emerson, author of "Self-Reliance"

Principle

Because both thoughts and feelings can be locked into our physical body, activities such as movement, body massage, and exercise can all serve to release these thoughts and feelings—freeing a person to higher levels of creative expression and full functionality. Rhythmic movements such as dancing, swimming, roller skating, walking, martial arts, and so on can not only facilitate the release of the thoughts within the body, but they can also serve to wire the brain in a more complex manner. Across the body, arm movements such as those used in swimming and vigorous walking serve to stimulate brain synchronization and complex synaptic development, which encourages bilateral development and better communication across the hemispheres.

Geriatric research demonstrates that those senior individuals who continue to maintain a flexible and supple body as a result of daily movement and exercise also maintain a more optimistic state of mind, as well as have a lower incidence of mental disease. This finding is in addition to all the other beneficial health effects of regular exercise.

Seeking ways to stay flexible also assists in reducing the effects of stress on the body and mental processes. Stress, as we discussed, produces chemicals and hormones that reduce mental effectiveness. Individuals seldom function creatively when under excessive stress. (Conversely, moderate stress or a sense of urgency has been shown to actually stimulate creativity when it does not create undue stress.) As the negative effects of stress accumulate—producing poor attitude, lack of sleep, loss of energy, depressed feelings, and so on—mental flexibility and creativity suffer. This bad stress, or distress, occurs when our emotional mind experiences unresolved feelings, or our body kinesthetic mind experiences overaction. It should be obvious that when the physical mind and emotional mind are not functioning optimally, the creative mind will reflect a similar performance lag.

Process

An easy way to facilitate a more flexible mental state begins with movement that stimulates external flexibility. One of the easiest methods I have discovered is spontaneous dancing and movements to music. Any time prolonged exposure to conditions that result in stressful feelings has occurred, you can practice a mental and physical cleansing with 10 to 15 minutes of this spontaneous dance movement.

Although many people are initially embarrassed or self-conscious about attempting the exercise, when the inhibitions are overcome and you begin to experience the results of the movements, the benefits will become immediately obvious. A complete description of spontaneous dancing appears at the end of the chapter.

Dancing, along with other physical movements, can be facilitative to the flexible, creative mind. It is important, however, that any movement chosen should be done freely, rhythmically, and with some spontaneity for the benefits to be maximized. Over-exercising or non-fluid forms of movement do not create the same result.

Using exercises devised by people such as human-development pioneer Jean Houston, psychologist Ida Rolf, and *Age Wave* author Ken Dychwald, people from all walks of life have experienced extraordinary mental, physical, and emotional changes, as well as dramatic changes in their attitudes and quantity of creative output.

Frequently, peak-performance individuals seek to dissipate their stress through high-intensity exercise. Endurance cardiovascular exercises or weight lifting often can be partially effective in reducing body kinesthetic stress. Intense exercise, however, is ineffective in managing unresolved emotional stress, although it can mask the symptoms.

Higher and higher levels of exercise can become their own stressful situation. Studies by physiologist David Neiman at Appalachian State University found athletes who ran more than 90 miles a week had a higher incidence of colds and infections than runners who completed only 40. The report also found that their levels of epinephrine and cortisol, which are destructive chemicals, were elevated from excessive exercise.[1] For maximum benefit and creativity enhancement, flexibility movement should be done moderately.

---

[1] Paul Keegan, "We Won't Let Him Hurt You," *Outside*, Volume XXIII, Number 2, February 1998, page 50.

Practice Exercise

Spontaneous Dancing

As the name implies, few rules should be considered when spontaneously dancing. Choose music that makes you feel, something that you can become involved in. Often I choose classical music, sometimes light jazz or New Age. Which style of music you choose is less important than selecting music that will influence your mood and stir you to movement. Push the furniture back away from the center of your room so you have an open area where you can dance. I usually recommend you attempt this alone the first few times, as most of us are a little self-conscious about our movements. Begin the music, allowing it to wash over you. Breath through your nose and exhale through your mouth as we discussed in an earlier chapter. Close your eyes and see the music in your mind. When you feel moved to do so, open your eyes and begin moving slowly with the sound. Imagine you are flowing, each movement fluid and smooth, and feel the sounds and experience the movement inside your body as you move outside your body.

In this exercise, you may choose to keep the music slow and fluid, or you can experiment with the music slowly accelerating until you find yourself dancing in an almost spontaneous frenzy. Should you choose to increase the music, do not overexert yourself—nor should you work to a peak and then stop. It works better to allow the music to begin to taper back to the slower, fluid pace that began your exercise. This cycle would be slow, faster, faster, fastest, slower, slower, and back to original speed. Initially, do not exceed 15 to 20 minutes for your dance. Later, you may choose to extend this to 30 minutes; however, you might be surprised to find that you lose all track of time and simply dance until you feel it is time to stop. Spontaneous dancing is a wonderful way to cleanse your being after a tiresome and mentally stressful day. You will be amazed how energized you are after the experience.

9

Relaxation fosters control.

"A relaxed person is a powerful person."
—Norman Vincent Peale

Principle

A few years ago, my oldest daughter and I drove half-way across America to take her to her freshman year at a Colorado college—just the two of us. I remember thinking of it as a last bonding experience for us before I lost her to the outside world. Although the trip was long and tiring, we talked a good deal and had several moments of outrageous laughter.

It was 9 p.m. after two full days of driving when we rolled up to the front of the dormitory. I was exhausted. She, at age 18, was impatient and wired. She found a resident assistant and located her room. It was on the third floor, the farthest point from the parking lot, and no elevator.

By the third trip up those stairs, I was becoming a little short-tempered. I was tired, my head and stomach ached, and I still had a 20-hour drive back the next day. I was near the point of temperamental "no return" when I got to the top of the stairwell. I stopped to rest, and pressing my boxes against a wall, I leaned against them. Inches from my face was a colorful poster some upperclassmen had created to cheer the arriving freshmen. It was one of my favorite Norman Vincent Peale quotes: "A relaxed person is a powerful person."

Someone once gave me a great definition for power: "knowing what you want to do and doing it." At that moment, I wanted to enjoy those final hours with my daughter, but when tension and exhaustion began eroding my attitude, my power began slipping away. Norman reminded me how to regain control: Relax.

A relaxed person truly is a more powerful person—powerful in that they have greater control over their outcomes because they utilize more faculties. They are also powerful because they can draw upon those resources more effectively and have greater awareness and insight into external conditions (and more fluid and fluent internal responses). They are more powerful because they gain and retain a greater amount of information in the process. And finally, they are more powerful because they enjoy the process more.

When you are not relaxed, it might be said that you are asleep to the possibilities of life. The busy mind, the mind preoccupied with doing and activity, is a mind that does not have the opportunity to become aware of the illusions of its thinking. The mind in repose, relaxed, or preoccupied with a triviality can be awakened.

Highly effective people are often functioning in a totally relaxed state. In sports we call this "the zone." When an athlete reaches a level of optimum performance, rather than maximum exertion, he or she seems to move into this almost meditative zone of relaxed peak performance. T'ai Chi master Chang Man-ch'ing observed that babies are born relaxed and yielding, but as they grow and become civilized, they are no longer relaxed. At birth it is intuitive for us to be relaxed in our efforts. Too soon we forget how to be in that relaxed mode and begin substituting tension, anxiety, and force.

Stress

When confronted with the challenges of life or when under pressure to perform, we often tense our minds and bodies in an attempt to focus on our goal or objective. This intense condition creates mental, emotional, and physical rigidity that causes us to be nonreceptive to the information and possibilities that surround us. We become inflexible, unconscious to other people and their feelings, as well as our feelings. This tension not only disempowers us, it blocks our ability to perform at our highest mental and physical levels. This rigidity eliminates flexibility.

Increasing tension often leads to the opposite of relaxation, which is increased stress. When under too much stress, most people undergo a measurable change in blood pressure, an increase in adrenaline, and an elevation in glucocorticoids, which are potentially destructive hormones. There may be an increase in respiration, perspiration, or even heartbeat. By the time you have become aware of these symptoms, the mental condition resulting from these circumstances has already firmly taken place. You have lost your control.

Remaining relaxed is the ability to maintain flexibility, centeredness, and balance, even when confronted with the most stressful of situations. Today's workplace is stressful. As much as 75 percent of employees' lost work days may be stress-related. The International Labor Organization reports that job stress costs the U.S. economy about $200 billion annually. Although learning these relaxation skills will not eliminate stress, you will discover ways to manage yourself so that stress does not become distressful.

The Only Time Is Now

Much of the anxiety and discomfort that degrades our present comes from our misunderstanding of time. There is only one time—the now moment. The moment you are experiencing is the only time you can ever experience— the only place you can participate. The past is a memory of the present, and dwelling on it can produce feelings of anxiety because you cannot do anything about the past. The future is anticipation of the present, and when you anticipate you often become fearful because once again you cannot act in the future. When you waste the present moment dwelling on the past or worrying about the future, it disempowers the present and makes you feel too helpless to act.

Time is not an external issue. It is an internal issue. Any attempt to manage time using external minutes, seconds, and hours is limited. The problem with time is our attitude about time. Learning to manage time is not about the past or future or what our watch or the clock says. Managing time is about being fully present in the moment.

Time becomes endless when you are centered in the present moment. When you lose the worries connected to past and the anxiety of the future, you become more productive because you begin to focus completely on what you are doing. Bringing your whole self into the moment is like sending in the reinforcements. It awakens the unconscious mind, revealing information, insight, and new patterns that might otherwise be elusive. Suddenly your entire creative being is available and engaged. Becoming centered in the timeless present frequently inspires the creative act.

Brain-Wave Patterns

Brain researchers have discovered, while measuring mental activity with PET scan technology, that those people who were most relaxed when problem solving, learning, or engaged in any form of mental activity utilized the largest areas of their brains in the process. Conversely, those who were tense, anxious, or concentrating too hard during the same tests used much smaller areas of their brains. The relaxed group generated more and better ideas more quickly and with less conflict.

Accompanying research has also shown that the more areas of the brain involved in processing events and information, the better the mental flexibility, recall, motor skills, and problem-solving abilities. As a plus, those subjects who were relaxed also indicated they enjoyed the problem-solving process more than those who were more tense or concentrating harder.

If you could see the brain-wave pattern of your relaxed centered mind, you would discover that the waves are smoother and more rounded than when they are in the tense or more fully alert mode.

In the alert conscious mode of awareness, you are generating an *electroencephalogram* (EEG) pattern called a beta wave. This wave pattern (in the 13- to 26-cycles-per-second range) is most closely associated with the active mental state, which is your usual awake alert condition. When the brain is engaged in some mental activity that requires alert attention, you will see these beta wave patterns. See Figure 9-1 for more information.

Alpha waves (in the nine- to 11- cycles-per-second range) are more smooth and rounded than the beta patterns. These waves occur at the first level of centered, or mindful, thinking and are associated with a more relaxed mental process. Although not asleep, people in the alpha state can often be less mentally alert to outer conditions as they are focused and preoccupied on their internal thoughts or external actions. See Figure 9-2 for more information.

Theta waves (occurring in the four- to eight- cycles-per-second range) are usually associated with a deeper relaxation state. Individuals under hypnosis, in deep meditation, or in a semi-conscious stage are usually in this theta wave state. The formative creative mind is most easily accessed when one drops into this theta state. See Figure 9-3 for more information.

Figure 9-1 Beta EEG Patterns
                13–26 cycles per second

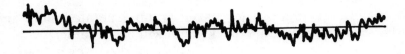

Figure 9-2 Alpha EEG Patterns
                4–8 cycles per second

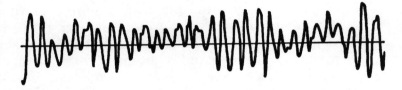

Figure 9-3 Theta EEG Patterns
                1–4 cycles per second

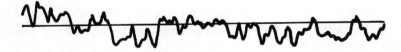

Menninger institute researchers Alyce and Elmer Green found in their research that most creative individuals appeared to be in the theta state while in their creative reverie. This state generated vivid, dreamlike pictures and visualizations that were like muses to the creative process.

"I began thinking about the possibility of developing a psychophysiological training for creativity," writes Elmer Green. "Deep relaxation plus theta feedback seemed a good place to begin. No matter how startling the notion might at first sound, there is reason to believe that a person can learn to be creative. Creativity does not have to be something you are born with (either you have it or do not have it), but [it] might be something that you can learn through theta training, training to control the focus of attention in a particular way. Perhaps everyone is innately creative and merely needs training in order to increase the objective evidence of it."[1]

Centering

Life accelerates, becoming more busy and more cluttered with action, activity, deadlines, and responsibilities. Keeping your center amid the distractions is important. In the contemplative traditions, returning to center means returning to the calm moment. Your center should be a peaceful place of reflection, calmness, and rejuvenation. Your practice should be one that complements your nature, either active or passive, mental or physical, and so on. As a wisdom enhancing tool, your centering practice can begin and end each day. Daily practice will open you to a broader understanding of the bigger picture, enabling you to take issues that challenge and confront you and see them from new points of view. From the center comes understanding, insight, and acceptance. Your centering practice is one of the most beneficial principles in achieving the fully functioning goal.

As responsibilities, workloads, and activity levels increase, so do the stressors. Stress, however, is simply demands made upon you, magnified by your lacking the coping skills with which to constructively handle those demands. Centering techniques provide powerful tools in dealing with external stressors. When you center yourself and bring your awareness into yourself, you can listen and look to see how you have been responding to

---

[1] Elmer and Alyce Green, *Beyond Biofeedback* (New York: Delta Books, 1977), page 124.

the events that surround you. Only then are you able to actively change how you respond, enabling you to restore a peaceful calmness in a relatively brief time.

Process

Teaching ourselves how to consistently respond in a relaxed way begins with understanding the principles of flexibility, centeredness, and balance, and then practicing them. These ideas may conflict with your previous programming, but new research is increasingly validating this wisdom. Practitioners are not only getting better outcomes but are also finding pleasure and enjoyment in the new consciousness levels of understanding that they have created.

If enhancing your mental performance is your goal, applying pressure will result in the opposite outcome. The more you try to relax, the less relaxed you become. Experience has taught us this lesson, although our logical mind might does always remember it. Concentrating too hard often only gets you a headache.

Take advantage of the mind's natural inclination to seek a solution or inspiration. When you relax, however, you sense and move naturally into the zone. This zone is always present, and it is only that our tense mind hides it from us; whereas relaxing reveals it.

The mind has an innate ability for "fuzzy" logic. "Fuzzy" logic uses the mind's auto-associative memory to associate seemingly random data. The mind generates an ongoing stream of possibilities at an unconscious level, which enables you to complete concepts or solve problems. This process fills in gaps in our thinking, anticipates possibilities based upon previous experience, and reconfigures new patterns when stimulated by random bits of information generated either internally or externally. The result of this process, when we allow it to occur, is a prolific output of ideas and possibilities that surround our situation or event.

Author Ken Dychtwald defines four stages of emotions. The first is tension. This stage is the initial conflict or problem. The second is charge. Charge is all the negative by-products of tension—chemical reactions in your brain or physical reactions in your body. You can be said to be charged when the initial problem or conflict is no longer immediate, but the emotions and physical effects remain. You must become aware of the tension and resulting charge before you can work through it to the third state, which is discharge. In this state, you can use any number of relaxation techniques to enable the original tension to work its way through your body. The result is Dychtwald's fourth state: relaxation.[2]

Remember, relaxing does not mean giving up your goal, slowing down, or stopping your effort. It simply means taking a less-rigid and less-intense pathway toward your objectives. This process not only invites higher performance but enables you to enjoy exactly where you are on the journey.

Centering

Point to your center. Your calm place within. Can you find it? Do you visit it often? Envision the eye of a hurricane—calm, quiet, and peaceful. Imagine the center of a wheel, unmoving, the radiating point from which movement occurs but which itself does not turn. The center of any object is the point from which all movements originate, but the center itself does not move. Being centered is bringing your awareness into the calm stillness within—the point from which your self originates.

The external world is a place of action, fast movement, deadlines, and hurriedness. To maintain your full functionality, you must not allow your internal world to become caught up in this frantic pace. Centering is bringing your awareness back to the calm and quiet moment of the present, back to your calm center. Centering brings your awareness into your self and the moment you are experiencing—the "right now." Centering brings your

---

[2] Ken Dychtwald, *Bodymind* (New York: Jove Books, 1978), page 120.

entire potential into that moment as well. Without the distractions of the external, your being is fully present to act.

Can you clear your mind and calm your center? While walking to a meeting for which you are late, can you practice being mindful of your walking rather than worrying about your punctuality? Can you do a breathing exercise or a relaxation technique after a difficult meeting? If you can, you are enhancing your life. Learning to center is about expanding your life moment-by-moment. Centering transforms how we process the moments that compose our lives, and it liberates us to calmly become more creative in the moments we have.

Breathing as a Centering Tool

One of the first techniques many people choose to begin in their practice of centering is diaphragmatic breathing, or deep breathing. Breath work can be very centering. Not only is it healthful and restorative, but it facilitates moments of insight and wisdom. It is also easily practiced at your desk, while on lunch break, when commuting (if you're not driving), or most anywhere you can find a few minutes to simply sit and breathe.

Standing or sitting in a relaxed position, place your tongue against the roof of your mouth behind the front teeth and inhale deeply through your nose for the count of four. The breath should fill the lower lungs or diaphragm first. Placing your hand at your navel will identify the base of your diaphragm. When inhaling, this lower area should inflate much like a ball. With practice, you can sense this inflation in your lower lungs. At the end of inhalation, your breath should be held for a count of seven, then slowly exhaled from the base of your diaphragm, through the mouth, for a count of eight. Inhale for four, hold seven, exhale for eight.

Many people have difficulty doing this simple breathing exercise. Initially, you may find this breathing technique feels unnatural. As you relax, with practice, this breathing will become easier and easier. You will be remembering. Watch a baby for additional instruction. This method is the way we all breathed as babies until we learned to breathe unnaturally.

Bring Your Mind, Body, and Feelings to the Same Moment in Time

I often explain to students that when the mind, body, and feelings are all in the same moment in time and space, a meta-awareness or heightened state of awareness occurs. Time seems to stand still. Your senses frequently become heightened; colors and textures seem more vivid; and smells and feelings become more intense. Many people observe that activities such as gardening, reading, playing music, and exercise can induce these deeper mindful stages. Complete attention to certain activities can become as transcendental and facilitative to the creative mind as sitting in classic meditation. The activity you choose often does not have to be a special one to provide this deeper mental state. The activity becomes special because of your mindful participation.

Allowing your distracting thoughts to fall away and becoming fully present in the moment in which you are participating becomes a reward in itself. You will notice things you might not otherwise notice. You will feel and sense your self and hear your body in a heightened manner. You will feel relaxed and peaceful. In this mindful state, your brain slows to the alpha and theta wave patterns. These patterns are essential to the creative state and the deeper thinking processes, in addition to being conducive to greater relaxation. During your practice of mindful activity, you will often find your mind discovering solutions to problems and gaining new insights into troublesome situations.

Meditation

Through meditation, you can also shift into the alpha and even deeper brain-wave state of theta. As you learn to mentally move to these states, the two hemispheres of your brain become harmonized. Research has shown that individuals who mentally become harmonized as a result of slowing to the theta state demonstrate increases in motor skills, language skills, sensory abilities, improved memory, concentration, and overall intelligence, and they also show better human relations as well as a higher creative problem-solving ability.

Dr. Robert Benson, author of *The Relaxation Response*, cites several meaningful changes that result from these mental practices. Among these are:

→ You can begin changing old bad habits.
→ You can alleviate many chronic illnesses.
→ You can alter unproductive ways of thinking and develop new disciplines that will help you realize your full potential.
→ You can embark on a truly transformed way of living.[3]

Many diverse activities can be effective in facilitating these slower brain wave patterns. Consistently, your best ideas or insights will occur when these lower frequency brain wave patterns are being created. While any non-logical activity that enables you to become centered and focused has the potential to be facilitative of these creative moments, meditation has been shown to bring more documented benefits than any other practice.

Moving Meditation

Every day in institutions throughout China, T'ai Chi and Qi qong practitioners pour by the thousands into the parks, lots, roof tops, and anywhere space permits. T'ai

[3] Herbert Benson, *The Relaxation Response*, (New York: Avon Books, 1975).

Chi and its parent Qi qong (where the practitioner visualizes energy moving in the body), are designed to align the internal and external mind and body and are also mindful practices. Research into T'ai Chi and Qi qong has shown they produce effects similar to biofeedback and meditation. These healthful exercises are as routine as the American coffee break, with a distinctive difference. These practices relax, calm, and improve the performance of the practitioners. Similar effects have been shown to occur with yoga movements and Sufi dancing.

When practiced regularly, simple techniques can bring about meta-normal beneficial changes both for the individual as well as the institutions they serve. More and more organizations and businesses in the United States have begun providing and encouraging participation in mindful practices, from meditation to T'ai Chi. Rediscovering the wisdom and discovering the benefits from these types of extraordinary centering forms may well be one of the more important discoveries of the next century. Growing our inner technologies to pace the growth of our outer technologies and developing our human resources as we have developed the natural resources will become the ultimate benefits of these consciousness evolving practices. If you have the time to make the commitment, seek out a teacher of a moving meditation form in your area. The World Wide Web or a local bookstore are great places to start looking for a teacher in your city.

Become Aware of Your Brain-Wave Patterns

Because brain waves do not produce sensory information that is detectable to the conscious mind, indirect forms of awareness are required to provide practitioners with the awareness of changes in these physiological states. Biofeedback devices can provide information regarding thought, emotion, and attention control. Biofeedback is learning to monitor awareness of your biology in a loop with consciousness, which feeds back information to effect a response. Developed as a consistently effective method of assisting individuals in alleviating psychosomatic illnesses, biofeedback enables you to receive tangible evidence of the relationship of the mind's control over many of the body's functions.

How does this relate to creativity? Biofeedback shows that the mind can create dramatic physical, cognitive, and emotional conditions. Studies done by Dr. Thomas Budzynski at the University of Colorado Biofeedback Center found that "when people were trained to achieve and maintain theta brain waves using biofeedback techniques, they did indeed learn much faster. Moreover, many emotional and attitudinal problems were solved at the same time."[4] Biofeedback provides a valuable tool for cross-training your thinking and performance.

A dramatic benefit, one most relevant to our cross-training interests, is that as the mind and body harmonize one area, other areas seem to be positively affected as a result. The Greens write that "many psychiatrists, medical doctors, and clinicians have observed in patients who used this training for self-regulation of physiological problems is that personality changes accompanied the psychological changes." The Greens go on to point out that as the physical condition changes, so do the emotional and mental states. "It is as if for each individual there is not only an ideal hemostatic balance in the physiological domain, but also an ideal hemostatic balance in the personality domain," they write.[5] Movement in one brings about movement in the other.

Because biofeedback practice results in the same brain-wave pattern changes as meditation and other mind-

---

[4] Colin Rose, *Accelerated Learning* (New York: Dell, 1985), page 24.

[5] Green, page 67.

ful practices, it deserves attention and study as a useful area for cross-trainers. Several methods of biofeedback measurement exist. In advanced workshops, I have begun experimenting with small hand-held thermometers enabling attendees to record their skin surface temperatures, which is an accurate biofeedback measurement tool. Simply holding the thermometer between the finger and thumb can result in an accurate measurement in a matter of moments.

Throughout the session, I regularly ask the participants to take a skin temperature measurement. Over a series of measurements, we come to realize that our temperatures do go up and down depending upon how relaxed we are. After a completely relaxing exercise, skin temperatures may be in the mid-90s. After a tense or stressful event, however, it might drop into the 80s. What we are doing is measuring the impact of events on the individual and recording the various responses our bodies demonstrate under different situations. As individuals learn to relax and become centered, their temperatures climb.

To consciously raise your body temperature, you might try a couple of activities. Visualize a warm feeling in the hands. For example, you might see the sun warming the hand and imagine that your hand is becoming warmer and warmer in the sunlight. You can also imagine the reverse—say your hand is in ice water, and you send warmth to it to reverse the effect of the cold water.

Biofeedback practice makes it easier to obtain and document higher and more constant levels of alpha and theta wave patterns. Although visualization is the primary tool used in conjunction with biofeedback, any number of anxiety-relieving exercises can have effects on your body temperature. As the theta level is achieved, the left brain harmonizes with the right—creating a synergistic harmonizing effect that accentuates your formative mind, creative thinking, and intuition.

Practice Exercises

1. Centering

Mindful sweeping is a practice that anyone can use to become more relaxed and centered. Choose an area to sweep that is large enough to allow at least 10 to 15 minutes for practice. Before you begin sweeping, hold the broom lightly and notice the weight and balance of the broom in your hands. Feel the smooth broom stick in your fingers. Bring your full awareness into the broom and feel of the broom as it makes contact with the floor. Begin sweeping almost as if you were moving water. Slowly and purposefully sweep the floor, being mindful of each breath and each stroke of the broom. Do not lean too far with the body or stretch any part of the body to its full extension; rather, use the entire body to make each movement. Turn always from the waist, using the arms and hands to direct the movement. Avoid flicking the broom bristles too harshly. Concentrate on each stroke and notice every detail of your actions. Do not rush to complete this assignment; rather, allow as much time as necessary to mindfully involve yourself in sweeping. If thoughts unrelated to the sweeping enter your mind, gently allow them to drift away and return your focus to the sweeping. After completing your sweeping, notice how clear and calm your mind feels. How long after the exercise do you retain this pleasant, calm feeling? What activity or event caused you to lose this feeling?

2. Meditation Exercise

Sit in a quiet place. Sitting early in the day or late in the evening seems to work best for most people. Rest your hands comfortably in your lap with your feet flat on the floor. (You certainly may sit in lotus or classic meditation form if you wish, but it is not necessary.) Become aware of your breathing. Observe your breath as it passes in and out of your nose. Allow your breath to drop deeper into your diaphragm, until your breath awareness starts and ends at a point just below your navel. Feel your body completely relax as you settle down. As you sit with your mind empty, observing your breathing, suddenly you will notice your mind has begun thinking about something. This process will happen without your awareness of when or how it began. You will simply suddenly notice that you are thinking about something other than your breathing. Good. This happens to everyone—even the most accomplished meditators. To return to meditation, first observe what you are thinking and acknowledge it mentally by recognizing it for what it is. For example, say to yourself, "Here I am thinking about paying my bills," or "Ah, I was worrying about my son's grades." Whatever you observe yourself thinking, see it, smile to yourself, and acknowledge what it is without judgment. Then, let it float away and return your mental awareness to your breathing. Each time a thought comes into your mind, repeat the process. Never become frustrated with the thoughts and do not give them any energy—just acknowledge them and let them float away. Always return to your breathing.

Sometimes a thought will persist by returning again and again. Do not give it any energy. "Hello again, my anger toward my spouse," you should say, or, "You're back, my worries about my promotion." Simply practice the process of letting go of the thought, no matter how many times it returns. Sit for at least 10 minutes each sitting for the first week. Sitting twice a day, in the morning and evening, can increase the effectiveness of the practice. The second week, you may increase your time to 15 minutes.

Over the course of several weeks, increase your sitting up to 30 minutes each time. You will notice that while thoughts continue to come, as a result of your practice you have become less concerned with them, and they dissipate more quickly. After a few sessions of meditation, you may want to get your notebook and record your thoughts or other observations.

3. Become Aware of Your Physical Reactions

Try this experiment for yourself. Take your pulse, body temperature, or blood pressure. Then watch the television news for 30 minutes. At the conclusion, retest yourself. What changes have occurred? Also note whether you are more relaxed and calm after viewing, or whether you are more uncomfortable.

4. Biofeedback

Become more aware of your body's reaction to stimuli by monitoring your skin temperature in multiple situations. Acquire a thermometer that can measure your skin temperature. I suggest you do not use a thermometer that is used to take internal temperature; rather, locate an outdoor thermometer. An indoor-outdoor digital version can be purchased for about $10 or $12 dollars and works great. Hold the sensing tip between the thumb and forefinger and practice visualizing the hand warming. As I have mentioned in this chapter, there are many different ways to actually generate a measurable result, and you may wish to practice with them to see which is most effective for you.

Journal Practice

Meditation

After a session of meditation, you may wish to answer some of the following questions in your journal:

→ Do you notice any patterns in the thoughts that are occurring?

→ Do some thoughts trouble you more than others?

→ How are those thoughts different?

→ How do you feel after a session?

→ Over a period of time, do you notice the patterns changing?

→ Are thoughts as insistent as they once were?

→ Do some thoughts return as often as they once did?

→ Have you noticed any behavior changes during other times of the day that you feel might be related to the practice?

→ Do you seem calmer?

→ Has anyone mentioned you seem more relaxed or pleasant?

→ Are you enjoying the sessions?

→ Do you find yourself looking behind events and seeing patterns and causes?

→ Is it becoming easier to separate your feelings from events?

10

Multiple answers always exist.

"We are victims of our culture to the degree that we are unable to see ourselves outside of it."
—Hayakawa

Principle

A few years ago while shopping at a large mall, I came across some elaborate, computer-generated art in a kiosk. Intrigued, I walked over and looked more closely. The small sign said the art was called "hollusions," and if I observed them, relaxing my eye muscles and letting my focus shift, a second image would be revealed. I stared at them for a few minutes. I tried squinting, then looking cross-eyed. I got closer, backed up, moved up, and moved down, but nothing happened. So, I tried harder.

I tried for several minutes to switch my brain into the proper mode for seeing, but no second perspectives were revealed to me that day. Because I did not understand what I was looking for, and I did not have an existing pattern to guide me as to what I might see, I was unable to relax my mind enough for a new visual to reveal itself. Some time later, while awaiting a plane in Atlanta, I saw another display of hollusions in the airport, and with nothing to do but wait on the weather, I bought a big frozen yogurt and stared at them awhile.

At first I tried forcing something to happen, I was looking hard for something to recognize. Then, remembering I was supposed to let my focus shift, I relaxed; slowing my breathing, I began to simply stare. I quit trying; I surrendered. Suddenly, an image extended outward toward me. It was as if I were being drawn into the picture. In an instant, I saw it. I blinked, and it was gone; the old graphic design was back. When I relaxed again, the new image came slowly back into view. When I realized the process, I had a new pattern that enabled me to see it, and by relaxing, I predictably enabled it to come. In short order, I worked my way around the kiosk and saw them all.

What happened? The art did not change; I did. By changing how I looked and eliminating my old context, I saw in a totally new way. We humans have binocular vision—two simultaneous representations of the world that merge the image into a third dimension. Your mind melds the multiple images into one that defines what you believe you see. But you can see the world in many ways.

The contexts through which you view and perceive your surroundings are constructs of society, social groups, religion, jobs, and so on. These cultural concept-precept (expectation-realization) arrangements are at work in everything from life expectancy to science. Rigidly adhering to fixed, limited perspectives eliminates both quality insights and the variety of one's experiences. Learning to become flexible and shift contexts can be illuminating during creative problem solving. Liberating your self from the point of view from which you initially look at a perceived problem enables you to see opportunities. Not only are multiple perspectives available in every situation, but it is also possible to have mutually exclusive right answers in the same situation.

Too often people hurry through life, only seeing what they are looking for and overlooking other points of view. You might say they are looking without seeing. When you look, the mind seeks information and data to fill in the outlines of the picture it already expects to see. Looking implies expectation. Looking is done with intensity and focus. Mentally anticipating, although useful in decreasing reaction time in crisis situations, also locks the anticipator into a sequence of expectation that eliminates all other possibilities.

Seeing, on the other hand, is looking without anticipation or expectation. More an exercise of mental relaxation than optic performance, it is an important tool for the creative person. Seeing provides for the possibility of surprise. In her book, *Drawing on the Right Side of Your Brain*, Betty Edwards writes that many people are poor artists not because they cannot draw but because "people never learn to see well enough to draw."[1]

Flexible Thinking

Flexible thinkers approach situations without preconception, even when they do not fully understand what they are getting into. They emphasize trying an approach (try-see) and seeing what outcomes occur. Practicing flexible thinking does more than simply solve the immediate problem. It helps you redefine your thinking to see problems from new perspectives. It shows you ways to look past your viewpoint and identify the even bigger, underlying issues. It can point the way to weaknesses in your old thinking and give you insights into how you might expand your thinking to embrace new possibilities.

---

[1] Betty Edwards, *Drawing on the Right Side of the Brain* (Boston: J. P. Tarcher, 1979), page 2.

The Western World View

As we discussed in Chapter 2, your world view is the underlying assumption about how the world operates, upon which all your ideas and philosophies are based. The mind of the West is much different than the mind of the East. Each mind has been developed upon assumptions, beliefs, and attitudes that have shaped what we term a world view. Your world view determines how your mind will self-organize the brain as it develops.

Much of the western world view has been shaped by seeking differences—separating and isolating elements, ideas, and things by reducing them to the smallest observable component. In the West, one seldom seeks the co-creational aspect (what is occurring at the mental level to result in these conditions) between things as much as they look for the cause and effect (what is happening outside me that is causing these conditions).

Born out of the model devised by the 17th-century scientist Rene Descartes, our world view separates the mind, body, and spirit through the process of reduction. Descartes' world view attempted to abstract events and things into smaller classifications—what makes this different than that, and so on. The western mind began dividing up the world into classifications and categories that represented this separating world view. A quick glance at a biological chart of phylum, families, and genus reveals this western science model at work through its observation and isolation of detail. This dualistic concept places elements in separate areas, allowing for little crossover, mutuality, or integration.

Institutions are comprised of people who have created a collective world view. Organizations that have dated world views have the same problems as people with dated world views: their perspectives are limiting their performance. Everything external is a manifestation of your internal perspective and your point of view. What begins on the inside with a thought is projected outside through visible action and attitudes, as well as invisible forces. The external world simply vibrates as a mirror of the internal world.

Organizational world views change when enough pressure is placed on the existing perspective to render it no longer functional, or when the organization becomes assimilated into a larger organization. Mergers and acquisitions often are simply the result of dated perspectives being eliminated through natural selection. As a case in point, today the average life expectancy of an American corporation is less than half that of a human being.

The Eastern World View

This reality believes all things are connected and relate to one another. This reality believes that the observed and the observer are one. It also believes that all things resonate with one another and are simply manifestations of the same thing. Rather than separate through dualism, this reality looks for the congruence, or the unity, of all things. It seeks the similarities and likenesses. This concept is the world view of the eastern mind.

The opposite of looking for differences is seeking similarities. When we look for similarities, we seek what we call *holons*. From the Greek holos (holistic and holy), holons are the broad similarities that distinguish the nature of things. The mind of the East is more oriented to holon-seeking. It does not separate into one perspective without recognizing complementary perspectives. The concept of Yin and Yang is fundamental in this thinking. Yin and Yang are not opposites, but rather are degrees of the same thing. Soft and hard, left and right, up and down, in and out—all things are defined within the extremes of their one nature, not separated natures. The binary operating system of your computer is based upon this Yin and Yang system. In binary mathematics, the one and zero signal two states of the same switch—on and off—that combine in such a way as to construct a new whole—a usable personal computer.

The concept of duality redefines our perception of problems, solutions, and right and wrong. These are no longer separate ideas, but they are extensions of one another. In the paradoxical eastern model, a problem coexists in every situation along with a solution. To express a problem is to express one perspective of a situation; to express a solution is to see yet another.

In no places are the differences in western reductionist thought and eastern holistic thought more obvious than in these two cultures' approaches to the practice of medicine. If the western mind reduces illness down to the smallest element and separates it from health, the eastern mind sees illness as a manifestation of the lack of balance within the system. The West approaches health care from the perspective of reductionistic specialities, while the East takes an approach from the systemic, big picture.

In the world of medical specialization, different medical specialists often prescribe different protocols of treatment for the same ailment. A surgeon sees an operation as the most obvious course of action. An internist sees medication as the answer to the situation. A psychologist might see the problem as mental. Is one of these practitioners right and all the others wrong, or are they all simply approaching the condition from the limiting perceptions of their specialized world view?

Many medical practitioners today are looking at both East/West models and asking whether perhaps together these approaches might suggest an even more enlightened world view. I heard Andrew Weil, a former fellow of the National Institute of Mental Health and the author of several books on health and healing, state at one of his lectures that the recovery rate of patients within all existing medical treatment protocols does not vary much, regardless of the mode of treatment used.

In some training and research institutions, medical students are now spending more time studying healthy people rather than simply probing and slicing open cadavers. Re-addressing the health question from the positive perspective acknowledges the question, "Why don't some people get sick?", rather than the historical question, "Why did someone get sick?" It is the same situation, but two different perspectives.

Dr. Larry Halverson, director of Cox Medical Center's Family Medical Care Center, observes, "Often in society things are interconnected. The same is true in family practice; illness is seen as a part of an interconnectedness to family and society."[2] The family practice movement is redirecting the health care provider toward the family where a condition of disease resides, rather than focusing upon the individual disease in isolation. This idea focuses upon the 80 percent of illness that a general practitioner can treat, rather than the 20 percent of the illness reserved for the specialist. This idea represents a major change in how the western medical mind is now seeing the condition of illness. Blending these East and West world view models of medical thought can result in stimulating yet an even more creative and enlightened new world view. Remember, new paradigm shifts encompass and further explain the older models. In other words, there are new rules, but it is the same game.

As in this example of the changing perceptions of health care brought upon by this merging of eastern and western minds, other areas of our lives might benefit from this exercise of broadening perspectives. Unfortunately, the self-organizing nature of our thinking excludes these possibilities without the provocation of some significant event. Since birth, we have been practicing our perspectives at the exclusion of all others.

When Buckminster Fuller demonstrated his first geodesic dome, he created a radical departure from the convention of existing construction. The geodesic dome, so different from most western conventional buildings, is still not widely accepted or built in the U.S. today. Fuller approached his structure from the perspective of dynamic tension, the holistic design where the symbiotic

---

[2] Used with permission, Dr. Larry Halverson.

relationships created the whole. In Fuller's model, you could not define one item without defining its relationship to the system. This process recognizes that the sum is far greater than the contribution of the individual parts, one tenet of Gestalt psychological theory. The result was an architectural design that used 20 percent fewer parts, required significantly less energy to heat and cool, and had greater design strength.

Fuller's formative, creative mind saw the opportunities by focusing upon the space within the structure, rather than the existing solids. Logical benefits recommend this new building structure, but old world views die hard. Even in the face of compelling evidence for change, you still do not see many domes in America.

Separating Thinking

Chungliang Al Huang, one of my T'ai Chi teachers, once asked the group to hold up our hands in front of our faces. "How many fingers do you see?" Most people of western education respond, "Five," because we separate the fingers from the spaces in between. Our mind has become trained to see the world in separation. We see the solids. A Chinese child, he tells us, sees nine: five fingers of solid, and four fingers of space.

Look at your hand. Do you see the nine fingers, five solid and four spatial, that comprise the whole? If you perceive that the space is necessary for the solids to exist, the solid fingers become no more a part of the hand than the space fingers. Each is part of the whole. It is always in the spaces where your creativity can take hold. Spaces reveal opportunities.

My mother used to tell me when I was a child, "Steve, sometimes you can't see the forest for the trees." We all know what she was referring to was my fixation on one specific aspect of an event that often blinded me to the larger event. The increasing specialization of a complex world, I believe, contributes to furthering this affliction.

Separation thinking reduces everything to its smallest element and then attempts to address it at this level. I call this Bark Vision. Specialists become so focused on their little spot of bark that they do not even realize it exists on a tree. Of the millions of doctorate holders in the United States alone, nearly all are unaware of most work being done outside their own specialty. When people become this removed from the big picture, they are in danger of operating at the level of intellect without intelligence.

An intellectual decision, although correct in a isolated sense, can be incorrect in a larger sense. A highly developed intellect can create a powerfully effective manufacturing process with a dangerously toxic by-product. The intellect can tell you that you are not responsible for the by-product, or worse—that it is not of interest to you. You are only responsible for doing your job, the success of your product. Our intellect somehow enables us to feel absolved of the repercussions of how the poison, or toxic process, is used or abused. This deluded thinking professes no responsibility for polluting the air or water as a result of its product development. When you operate with the separating world view perspective, you fail to see the connectedness of things. It is easy to become hypnotized by your point of view, and without motivation to change, cling to it your entire life.

Creative formative thinking is always intelligent. It focuses upon the bigger picture constantly working to encourage a larger, more inclusive perspective. Rather than reduce and separate, it attempts to connect, relate, and associate. You are continuing to uplevel your vision and perspective.

Convergent Thinking

The convergent thinking style of our linear left hemisphere teaches us to choose the one right answer. It does not ask us to go any further than one right answer. Our divergent thinking right hemisphere stimulates us to look beyond a simple answer and seek other possibilities. It also encourages us to question the question, or at least question how we are stating the question.

The question is not about finding the right answer, but rather, "How do I find more answers?" Often there are many possible right answers. Pick some. After thousands of quizzes and tests to find one right answer in school, we have been conditioned to seek only one right answer in life. This process restricts our ability to look for other possible solutions. It also inhibits the utilization of other senses and processes in the decision-making matrix.

Process

Flexible thinkers have in common the characteristic of accessing their whole brains. Using all aspects of their minds—emotional, physical, logical, and intuitive—enhances this flexibility. Often, although unformed in the conscious mind, ideas can be released or channeled through other modes of expression associated with these diverse minds. Using movement, play, music, art, storytelling, visualization, and so on creates access to our greater mental potential. When these moments occur, we are often not aware of them at the time because we are so engaged in our actions. Our self-conscious criticizing mind is not involved in the process. After such an experience, the writer or artist might say, "I don't know where that object or idea came from. It just seemed to appear while I was painting or writing."

Change Your Perspective

Mental flexibility is necessary in order for the mind to move nimbly from fixed thoughts to multiple possibilities. In doing so, the mind operates in a lateral thinking mode, exploring a panorama of options in a non-judgmental way, rather than exploring one avenue of thinking in critical detail. This approach is a process of the right hemisphere—the pattern-generating hemisphere of our brains.

In order to see something for which you do not have an existing pattern, you must enable your formative right hemisphere to construct a new pattern or patterns. This event can occur by constructing new thought processes or by simply rearranging existing processes in a new, insightful order. This effect can be stimulated by shifting your focus onto some other arrangement of the information, which can challenge your perspective and reveal new patterns.

Many of our most profound insights occur when something we have seen and felt we understood in one way is suddenly viewed from a new perspective. Sometimes the new perspective is brought on by age or maturity. Sometimes the context in which the perspective occurs can present the information in a slightly altered manner and affect the insight. Various methods can be used to stimulate this process.

In their efforts to stimulate creativity, many organizations are seeking more creative practices to challenge managers to get outside their box. Trainers seeking to stimulate flexibility, and hence, creativity, are often looking outside the conventional offerings for employee training. River rafting trips, rope mazes and puzzles, simulated crises in space or aboard ships—even trips to the Discovery Zone—provide for these paradigm-shifting experiences. When we find new ideas and insights from experiences and events not bound by habit and fixed attitudes, they often present creative possibilities and mental switching opportunities in more acceptable and easily comprehended ways. Simply changing where we are when we are doing the thinking can have a profound effect on the thinking process.

Sometimes, your environment can provide new ways of understanding the true nature of the problem so you can be more creative in your solutions. I often ask seminar attendees to lie on the floor while brainstorming, or I take them outside to a park, arcade, or mall for a creative session. Environment shifting and changing your relationship to the problem can make a significant difference in how you see, and hence, how you think. Changes of place create a variety of stimuli, which interacts with the information and creates the possibility of seeing new patterns by contextually shifting the environments where the thinking is taking place.

When I was remodeling a building to accommodate our advertising agency a few years ago, one of the areas we were required to address was making the facility Americans with Disabilities Act-compliant. We needed to ensure that access was available for physically challenged individuals, both into and throughout the building. In one of the closets, I found an old wheelchair that had been left behind by a previous tenant. One evening I pulled out the wheelchair, dusted it off, and sat down. Confining myself to the wheelchair's limitations, I set out to navigate our building. There is no comparison between the revelation that took place from that experience and the information I gained from reading the ADA literature. Sitting in the wheelchair, I became informed of the problem when I became ensconced in the problem. When I changed the context of my thinking by changing my experience, I changed my way of understanding of the problem.

Create a Playful Atmosphere

Sometimes I find that a quick way for creating an environment for maximized creative thinking is creating a playful, or game-like, atmosphere. In brainstorming sessions, for example, I often introduce Nerf toys and other toss-around toys that cause individuals to pay attention to the play. Individuals are asked to say the first idea that pops into their mind when they catch a ball or a paper airplane. Frequently, the ideas are surprisingly relevant, and, because they are spontaneous, often clear and responsive.

Using another practice called spotlight singing, one person steps to the imaginary spotlight on the floor and begins singing to a popular melody, some improvised lyric loosely related to our problem-solving session. At any point, the facilitator points to a second individual who quickly jumps to the imaginary spot and continues the song where the other person stopped. This activity can continue for several minutes and often results in wonderful insights and ideas that can be built upon.

Occasionally I ask attendees to draw a problem, or sketch a solution, utilizing their artistic feelings to guide the imagery during the creative thinking session. Complex issues can often be dramatically simplified and clarified using this technique. Color choices also have profound meaning in interpreting the visual creations. Because visuals and art speak to us in non-literal ways, the creativity expressed by the artist and understood by its viewers often provides transcendent insights and stimulation that exceeds the possibilities provided by language.

Finally, storytelling using only one word at a time is a favorite of creative-thinking teams who are looking for ways to break their patterns and get outside the mental traps of habitual thinking. In this exercise, the group provides a title to the story and/or plot and characters, and then enables the story to literally tell itself as each of seven people only say one word at a time. It is best if the storytellers line up and tell the story one word at a time from left-to-right. With practice, the participants become quite adept and quickly learn to end sentences abruptly, repeat important information, and say the first word that comes to mind. This exercise can also be created using a flip chart, with each person writing one idea at a time. The experience of this exercise completely rewires the thinking and perceptions of the issue being discussed and opens the doors for a flood of creativity and energy afterwards.

In each of these examples, play was used as a constructive tool to provide stimulus for mental shifting and flexibility. Whether through music, rhythm, visuals, or physical activity, the right hemisphere was engaged— and the shifting that occurred facilitated the desired outcome of more, unexpected, and diverse ideas in situations that otherwise resisted fresh approaches. You can achieve the same outcome individually by practicing with switching techniques when working on a thinking-outside-the-box issue.

Practices that accentuate this process involve moving while you are thinking, listening to music, or daydreaming. Experiment shifting from your problem-solving activity to organizing files, doodling, or playing with toys. Switch from seeking a new idea to balancing your checkbook or organizing your office. After mulling over a personal problem, try doing a little housework, mowing the lawn, or washing dishes. Consciously moving from linear to non-linear activities, or mentally complex to simple activities, can be both stimulating and insightful. Often when alternated, these activities create the possibility of the "ah-ha" of insight—because you are breaking your existing patterns or routines.

Context Shifting

Yet another variance of this process is the practice of context shifting, which means actively shifting the contexts, environments, or conditions where you see events occurring. Context shifting enables you to place new backgrounds behind events by using your imagination to place the issue in a new setting. Taking a problem out of the workplace and placing it in a new environment, or considering a process from the perspective of a different type of organization or industry, often empowers new points of view.

Look at the illustration in Figure 10-1. What do you see? If you see the object as small, in the context of peering through a microscope, perhaps it is an amoeba. If you are looking down from a high place, as in the context of a hillside or hot-air balloon, perhaps it is a golf green, even higher as from an airplane, an island. If you were looking up, perhaps from the perspective of an ant, you might see the sole of a shoe. Is it a potato with an eye, a bean, a water balloon about to hit your face, or an enormous nose with the other facial features too large to be captured on the available background?

In each example, you did not actually manipulate the image you were seeing as much as you manipulated the context in which you imagined you were viewing it. The practice of playing with contexts can be profoundly flexing, because it enables you to bring into the equation far more ideas and stimuli. By combining context shifting, alternating your focus from the holistic, big picture, right brain to the algorithmic, linear left, far more possibilities appear. Because the right brain seeks ambiguity, fantasy, and metaphor, and the left looks at more detailed, logical, specific elements, this simple alternating process can release mental rigidity. It is like scanning from foreground to background, impression to detail, color to shape or form, center to sides, and so on.

Figure 10-1

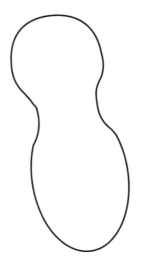

Possibility Thinking

One of the earmarks of creative people is that they do not get stuck on their first right answer. They go on to a second, a third, a fourth, even a 20th or 50th answer. Although many of the answers you initially generate may work to solve the immediate problem, they may not inform you to go beyond the problem and ask deeper, more probing questions. Designating your first workable answer as "the solution" prevents you from finding even better solutions to that same problem.

Instead, try to ask yourself questions that search for possibilities. What else could I do here? How would I solve this if I were the customer, not the provider? What would we do if our new solution failed, and we needed yet another answer? How might we solve this if we were in a different industry? What other types of businesses have a problem like this? What have they done? What opportunities does this problem present me to rethink our service or retool our product? Possibility thinking can be endless.

Rephrase the question, "How do we get rid of the extra people after a merger?" into, "How do we find productive things for all these new people to do?" and view the situation in as many different ways as possible—the more the better. Look for different contexts where the problem can be stated. Then, seek as many possible answers to each question as you can. Reverse the situation. Change "How do we ship our product to the customer more quickly?" into, "How do we get the customer to order further in advance or want it more slowly?" or, "How do we assemble it at the customer's location or get them to assemble it?"

Create a World View of Commonality

Let's superimpose a new world view. In this world view, all aspects of the whole are connected by a commonality—

a commonality of vibration. Imagine everything you perceive is the same matter and is simply vibrating at varying frequencies. Living cells vibrate, and particles vibrate. Both physicists and biologists are, at present, working with ideas that reflect a simple hypothesis that at the smallest level, life vibrates or resonates much like the strings on a stringed instrument. In this world view, all elements of the known universe, at their smallest level, vibrate in the same manner.

Perhaps you have experienced the effects of walking into a meeting or office that seemed charged with negative energy, where the room or space seemed to be heavy with negative vibes. Or perhaps while walking in the woods or by a stream, you felt a sense of calm and peacefulness. Undeniably, space contains and emits this vibratory energy.

This vibrational explanation can be validated within the eastern tradition as well as the western, and even through such divergent world views as the Aboriginal songline culture. This vibration world view could also explain many things that do not fit into our existing mental models of understanding. Perhaps as a child's mind begins to vibrate at the frequency of language development, it is harmonizing with the already-present cultural language vibration.

Whether or not this explanation works for you is not important. What is important is that by challenging your world view, you open your mind to new expectations. Perceptions of situations significantly shift, contributing to changes of expectation that result in new possibilities. If everything is vibrating and sending you information at a vibrational level, then suddenly things such as intuition and informative feelings are much more easily explained. If more acceptable, you may begin to act upon them in a new, more conscious manner. The result is that you get new outcomes you have never before experienced, all of which make sense to you now from this newer, larger perspective.

Allow for Contradictions

"At 4 a.m., Ed Lark, a member of the geographic team, measured the coals with an optical pyrometer from the Ceylon Institute of Scientific and Industrial Research. The pyrometer registered 1,328 degrees Fahrenheit," writes Joseph Chilton Pearce of the 20-foot fire pit prepared for a ritual fire walk. "Nearly 20 people, men, women, boys, and girls, walked the fire. Some walked it several times—they showed no sign of any blisters or burns."[3]

How do you react to those occurrences that contradict your perceptions? Doubtfully? Distrustingly? Fearfully? What do you do when the information you receive does not fit any pattern you hold, or worse yet it contradicts the patterns you hold dearly? Ignore it? Argue against it? Perhaps you don]t even notice it.

If you do not reconcile and reframe new information into a larger world view, you are left to simply reject it. Doing so, you lose the opportunity to uplevel your knowledge, skills, thinking, and experience. You cannot force these contradictions with your logical mind. What you can do, however, is allow them. By enabling your right hemisphere the opportunity to graze the information uncritically in expectation of discovering a new pattern, you can reframe the information into something understandable, which leads you to more enlightened thinking. In other words, we are talking about productive results, not destructive results. Enabling a new paradigm to be crafted does not have to call into question the principles of the previous paradigm—only our understanding of those principles.

Understanding that these different perspectives exist is vital if you are to open your perceptions to new models of thought, action, and prosperity. Our western-thinking paradigm is one model, and the eastern is yet

---

[3] Joseph Chilton Pearce, *A Crack in the Cosmic Egg* (New York: Julian Press, 1971), pages 101–102.

another. Although neither can be completely right, neither can one be completely wrong. Understanding these two different approaches and drawing upon both to synthesize a higher level of interpretation is a process of cross-training. Placing less emphasis on what you are now and more on what you could become shifts you to a more enlightened awareness. Recognizing the power of the contradiction of processes and looking for the insight from that, continues your growth in the direction of wisdom. As each of us becomes wiser, we all become wiser. That is the way of full functionality.

Practice Exercises

1. Take a Mini-Retreat

Find time this week for an afternoon nature mini-retreat. Locate a quiet setting outside the city where you can get away from the noise and crowds. Often you will find hiking trails, natural parks, conservation areas, or state parks just a few miles away. Take the day trip alone, or with someone who enables you to be alone, and get out and walk. After you have walked a while, seek a quiet place where you can sit and watch nature unfold—perhaps on the bank of a stream or on a hilltop. Observe what happens in nature. Do not think too much about the activities that unfold around you or get too lost in your own day dreaming. Simply watch nature, observe the detail of life around you, become aware of your senses, and enable yourself to experience the day and your surroundings in as open a manner as possible. See what happens when you use all your senses. Open yourself to the possibility of experiencing the vibration of your setting. Sometimes the vibration becomes more noticeable when you return to the faster-paced environment which contrasts it.

2. Flexibile Thinking

A. Try looking at things in different settings.

→ Take a mental picture of a problem and move it outside.
→ Take your problem-solving meeting to a museum.
→ To create more flexible thinking, get up and move.

B. Take a lunch walkabout. Bring your lunch with you to work for a few days when the weather is pleasant, and slip on your comfortable shoes and zip out the door—lunch in hand—for an hour walkabout. Pick a pathway that does not bring you into contact with much traffic. This might mean you will have to drive a short distance to get to a quieter area. In inclement weather, you can do this at an indoor mall. Begin your walkabout with the awareness of your breath and centering that we have discussed previously. Then, set out with an open-to-whatever-you-encounter-observant mental attitude. Do not allow yourself to become too distracted by the things you see; however, always be vigilant to see everything you can. Do not judge or evaluate anything, nor should you become too involved in thinking about anything. Simply keep your mind open and observant. Allow things to pass by your mind in much the same way they pass by your body. With regular practice, many people find this not only relaxing but highly generative with regard to discovering ideas or solutions for problems or issues with which they are currently dealing. Often these ideas seem to magically appear when our mind is clear and open. Always carry a notepad so you can jot down any ideas you have; then continue the walkabout with the understanding you will go back to that idea later when you return to work.

3. When Faced With a Disagreement

A. Try to focus on a common element and direct your attention and their attention to that area of agreement. For example, you might say, "OK, well, I notice we both agree that the new person should have some front-line food service experience. What are your thoughts on the type of service experience?" Keep the questions flowing.

B. Practice focusing upon the other person, not simply the area of disagreement. Look for something about them you genuinely like. Listen and sense them mindfully.

C. Look closely at their point of view. How do you suppose they came to their conclusion? Do any aspects of their perspective make sense? Is there a third perspective that would either result in agreement, or, at a minimum, avoid conflict?

D. Look at the big picture. Ask what is the ideal outcome for everyone in this situation, not simply your ideal outcome.

Journal Practice

Flexibility Questions

→ Which areas of your life have become inflexible due to a fixed point of view?

→ Are there certain individuals that you seem to have more differences of perspective with than others?

→ Why is it easier to see alternatives when you are not directly involved in the problem?

→ What points of view do you currently hold about yourself that are limiting your growth and creative potential?

Success is moderation
in all things.

"If consciousness is the mere impotent shadow of action, why is it more intense when action is most hesitant? And why are we least conscious when doing something most habitual?"
—Julian Jaynes

Principle

I have a friend who leads executive retreats for senior managers and chief executive officers from large organizations all over the world. During his programs, he asks attendees to question their lives in rather revealing detail. During one such session, he told me about a participant who broke down as he discussed his situation. This CEO of an organization with annual revenues to rival a small country found himself growing farther and farther away from his only son. They were no longer able to talk without arguing. He feared his son was having some real problems at an important time in his life. The man confessed that he knew his career demands were a core issue in their relationship problems.

A few weeks after the retreat, the man was offered the position of international CEO for the organization. This position would entail his moving to Europe. He turned down the promotion and made the decision to leave the company, citing family issues.

What this man really decided was to choose his son over his career. He was not willing to drag his son to yet another city. That decision required a reprioritization of his life, putting family at the top of his values again. My friend says he talks with the man often, and he now has a successful second career that demands much less of him. His relationship with his son has dramatically improved.

This story is not unique. Lack of balance between work and personal life is one of the top six reasons new managers leave their positions. I saw the results of a recent study that indicated making money was no longer most people's number one motivator. Among working women who also managed families, this study reported that the women would rather simplify and have more time for their lives in exchange for monetary gains.

This same attitude is being reflected by more and more disenchanted baby boomers who are exchanging stressful lifestyles for more balanced lives. We all know someone who has forfeited a big salary in order to pursue a dream, have more time with the family, or get back in touch with their lives. Peter Lynch resigned at the top of his game. The North American president of Pepsico, Brenda Barnes, stepped down, citing a desire to spend more time with her family. An attorney friend of mine took a one-year sabbatical from his firm to spend time with his ailing father. When his father passed away, he never went back. Today, he practices out of his home.

Cultural Pressures

How we balance our lives and still strive for success is an individual matter. How do you define success? Is it an important job, a big income, a fine home, a good family, a rich spiritual life? Asking these questions of people, we discover not everyone responds in the same way. Even so, cultural pressures lead many to define success narrowly.

Our culture is enamored with the material aspects of success. Making money, acquiring "stuff," and amassing a fortune are quite clearly what too many people perceive as "making it" in America. Businesses focus too heavily on achievement, gain, and profit. You must make money, work hard, and make more money. Life is expensive. You can never get enough. We always need more. We need bigger houses, newer cars, and more stuff. Improve the bottom line. We have all been caught up in it at some level.

The sacrifices required to acquire these outward rewards often cause one to make value and ethical decisions that have long-term consequences on one's well being. The quest for external things ultimately does not satisfy us. You cannot satisfy your internal cravings with external junk food. We constantly find ways to rationalize our choices. As Jeff Goldblum's character observed in "The Big Chill," we cannot get through the day without a big, juicy rationalization. Rationalizing has become a defining characteristic of our situational culture.

Our conscious, analytical mind blocks us from our true feelings and attitudes. This left hemisphere mind focuses on ego, getting things, and gratifying our needs. Addictive behavior is born in the conscious ego mind. It deludes us into believing the compromises we make will not affect or change us. We somehow feel we can fix it if we discover later that we have given away too much. But as individuals and as a culture, these rationalizations bring us more out of balance.

Process

Too often it has taken a revolution to overthrow an out-of-balance government and replace it with a new one. Individually, it frequently takes a crisis before we make the necessary course corrections in our lives. We over-balance one aspect until it becomes untenable, and we then abandon that course for an entirely new direction. These radical responses are not usually effective methods of change, because they often come too late. They stress the system in their implementation, and the radical changes meet with strong resistance. Effective change is slow and continuous.

Know Your Priorities

One evening while driving across Iowa, I was listening to the audio version of Brian Tracy's "Psychology of Achievement." He was discussing a simple exercise for getting in touch with our feelings. "Write down the five most important things in your life," he said. The question was so profoundly simple and thought provoking that I pulled over to the side of the highway, turned on the dome light, and got out a notebook and a pen.

My answers did not come quickly, but when they came, they came from inside me. I knew when I finished writing down five items, they were real. I then turned the audio tape back on and heard Tracy ask, "How much time are you devoting to those five items on your list?"

You know it is time to make changes if the majority of your time is devoted to something inconsistent with your values. If you are postponing your life in order to get ahead or setting aside your values to gain a little more, you are out-of-balance. Out-of-balance people do not operate at their best. More importantly, they rob themselves of their true happiness. Balancing brings us back to ourselves.

Do Not Exchange One Obsession for Another

My friend Rita Gurian, who started The Women's Center at a large Midwestern hospital, gave me a little booklet several years ago containing the 15 components conducive to well-being. I took the accompanying test, thinking I would probably do pretty well. I really bombed in the areas of nutrition and taking time to appreciate my accomplishments. Balance, I discovered, is not exchanging one obsession for another. It does not come from transferring our compulsions and additions to new choices. Excess in the name of virtue still is not healthy. Balance is moderation of all things, and it is old wisdom we have been ignoring too long.

A few years ago, my business career begin to dominate my life. I was ignoring my family, my body, and myself. Realizing this, I decided to make several changes. In the area of health, I knew I was not getting enough exercise, so I decided to make the commitment to get into shape. As a high achiever, I needed a powerful goal to keep me going to the gym everyday. I decided to compete in a triathlon.

I began training with a vengeance. I spent hours running, working out on stairmasters, and pedaling my bike up and down hills. I built up my legs and my gluteous maximus until I was as hard as a statue. I also ruined my posture, pinched a nerve, and developed sciatica. All I had done is exchange one obsession for another. I was still out of balance.

The Tao teaches the concept of the middle way. The middle way is centered upon not giving too much or taking too much of ourselves from any one thing. We balance by spreading ourselves across many things. Integrating the diverse aspects of balance provides harmony in our lives. It creates for us the opportunity to live fully with all aspects of our humanness, rather than attempt to filter all the joy life has to offer through the narrow pathway of one channel.

Like Darwin's theory of biological diversity, the broader the sources, the healthier the system. If we give too much of ourselves to any one thing, we create the likelihood of eventual disappointment. The secret to greater fulfillment is seldom increasing our quantity of one thing. It is rather increasing the variety of things from which we compile our self-identity—or cross-training.

Think of it as personal diversity. How diverse are you in your life? Do you find time on a weekly basis to spend time with loved ones, exercise, and work on your hobbies? Do you strive toward goals, keep mentally stimulated, and still find time to walk in the woods occasionally? Everyone has his or her own mix of priorities, but it is important to ensure you have and honor yours. Consider them your adult requirements for balanced living. We do not all need the same things in equal measure, but for the most part, all humans require balance if they want to maintain happy, healthy, enjoyable lives.

Balance also enables us to release our creativity, both directly and indirectly. It works directly by providing the variety of activities whereby we can practice our creative expression—hobbies, art, crafts, outside interests, and so on. Indirectly it provides us the release of our creative energies that are often stifled when we become too one-dimensional.

Balance in the Organization

Becoming more fully functioning as individuals causes us to begin looking for ways to make our institutions and organizations more fully functional as well. Businesses are really living entities—organizations comprised of smaller living parts. The whole is greatly dependent upon the well-being of all these parts. Living organisms that are healthy are also comprised of healthy parts.

I remember years ago my first visit to Tyson Foods. I was standing in the lobby with an associate, and we were waiting for the person we had an appointment with to come and meet us. An average-looking gentleman in brown pants and a brown work shirt walked into the lobby. His dress instantly made me think he must be the custodian or something. He noticed my associate and called him by name. They both smiled, shook hands, and exchanged pleasantries for a moment, and then my friend turned to me and said, "Steve, meet Don Tyson."

Here was the chief executive officer of the largest food company in the world, and I thought he was the janitor. We talked for a moment. He was friendly, comfortable, and down-to-earth. Clearly, he was not a man impressed with power ties. Later, when we met our client for the appointment, he was dressed in the same way as Don Tyson.

Often in entrepreneurial companies, regardless of size, you will see unique value structures that break the convention. They might be in dress code. They might be in organizational structure. They might be in job description, and so on. Over the years, I have worked as a consultant with a wide and diverse variety of companies, and I have come to the conclusion that there is not a right or wrong model, structure, or convention that will assure success or guarantee failure. I have met bankers with pony tails and bankers with crew cuts, and both were successful.

Regardless of their style or structure, the one thing that seems consistent in companies that continue to grow and prosper is that they also encourage their people to grow and prosper. Organizations are only as effective as the people who comprise them. And people who are spiritually, emotionally, and intellectually aligned with their companies are the soul of modern commerce. The good companies care about their people, and as a result, their people care about the company and the company's customers.

Historically, business has used profit as the measurement of success. A survey of many of the most successful companies over the past 50 years, however, reveals a more enlightened corporate picture. Of the 18 most visionary companies in this study, 16 had three or more references in their mission statements to well-being. Only six percent of these companies mentioned corporate profits and shareholder value in their value statements. All these companies had a strong core ideology: values plus purpose. These same companies, however, had 15 times greater shareholder returns than the general market over a 60-year period. Arie de Geus, author of *The Living*

Company: Habits for Survival in a Turbulent Business Environment, states that economic companies, which base their decisions on short-term financial concerns, do not live nearly half as long as living companies, which base their decisions on the company's and employees' potentials as a living entity. Between 1970 and 1983, one-third of the Fortune 500 industrials vanished.[1]

Fully functioning people create fully functioning organizations whose values reflect theirs. This harmonizing of personal and professional mirrors the growing integration of ourselves and reflects a rejection of the old dualistic paradigm of separation of work and life, personal and professional. Our discomfort with rationalizing our choices is demonstrated in an explosion of small business that are being created to reflect the values and attitudes of the entrepreneur. A new generation of workers entering the workplace are also demonstrating these attitudes as an important aspect of their decision matrix. Many today are seeking work that complements their lives, without consuming it. At job interviews, they are interviewing the companies regarding the organization's flexibility for independent work and lifestyle habits, training opportunities, human and environmental values, brain and body healthy programs and attitudes, and integrity.

Practice Exercise

The Nature of Balance

Here is an easy exercise to experience the subtle nature of balance in a physical environment. One of my first lessons in T'ai Chi class is standing with balance. First, stand comfortably with your feet at shoulder width, knees

---

slightly bent, and your posture relaxed. Feel the weight of your feet on the floor, from your toes to your heels. Now, step out with your right leg 18 to 24 inches, or until the heel of the right foot is just past an imaginary line running in front of the toes of your left foot. Maintaining that shoulder-width stance, with the front knee more bent than the back, slowly pour your whole body forward. Do not lean out; rather, keep your erect stance. When your front knee is above the toes, stop. Looking down on your right knee, you should see a bent knee directly above, flat toes, and everything all pointed the same direction. If you do, you should be balanced in this position. Your back foot is still flat on the floor. This movement is one of the J'ai Ji stances. If you enable your knee to move any further forward past the toes, you begin to feel off balance. The further your knee passes past your toes, the more your balance begins to falter—until you either have to step forward to recover, or you jerk back to regain your balance, in which case you overbalance the opposite direction. This simple exercise is a microcosm of most of our lives. If leaning forward feels good, we ask, why not lean farther? Nature has a way of correcting our mistakes.

Journal Practice

Balance

1. Sit down and make a list of the things that are most important to you. Where do you get your greatest happiness? What do you enjoy spending your time doing? Who do you most enjoy being with? Which activities give you the greatest sense of personal satisfaction? You decide.

After you make your first list, fold it, put it in a prominent place, and forget about it. One week later, sit down with a second piece of paper and make a second list of the most important things in your life. Rank them. Then pick up the first piece and open it up. Are they the same?

2. How much time are you spending with the items on your list? What are the areas where you are out of balance? Devote one or two mornings of writing to address the balance of your life. What can you do to improve your life balance? Who can help?

3. Practice making a list of all the things you have to do one day each weekend, then start taking things off. How many can you eliminate? Can you eliminate them all? If so, you can play that day. Nearly all of us can use a day of play.

12

Cross-training is important to the new workplace.

"Now is the time for society to turn to developing inner technologies ... the untapped potential of the human mind for individual and collective creativity."
—Jon Kabat-Zinn

Speaking at the San Francisco Commonwealth Club in April 1997, Steven Covey asked the audience in the crowded Nikko Hotel ballroom, "How many of you believe that your people are far more intelligent, capable, and creative than their jobs enable them to be?"[1] Nearly every hand in the room went up. Although the response should not be surprising, what is surprising is that in a country that admires creativity so much, so little is being done to cultivate it.

Change begins from the inside out. As you and I become more creative and fully functioning, the pressure

---

[1] Used with permission from The Covey Institute.

179

increases to create more fully functioning organizations. Those of us in the business world need not only to be prepared for the changes, but we need to be involved in encouraging changes that enable organizational models emphasizing the human potential.

The successful organization of tomorrow will be much like the geodesic dome, in which all parts become dependent upon each other, and the structure is only as strong as its weakest component. What a business does and its environment are less important to its structure and survival than how a business thinks and changes. What we think and believe will become what we produce. In organizations, the quality of the thinking will become your most vital resource, profitably creating and producing in environments of fulfillment and stimulation.

The new manager must recognize that everyone in the organization must operate at his or her highest ability if the organization is to achieve its maximum potential. The manager must strive to create a motivating environment in which this can come about through the empowerment and participation of everyone involved.

Remember, the organization is made up of individuals —many of whom are unaware of their own limitations. Awakening and releasing the creativity within the organization will require the practice and implementation of the same individual cross-training principles discussed in this book. The difference is that you, as a manager, are challenged to aid the awakening of those individuals who make up the organization through your actions and the environment you create.

Let's revisit Carl Rogers' five conditions necessary for creativity (found in Chapter 1, which discusses the elements of creativity) for a model on which we can base this organizational change.

Openness to Experience

Openness to experience is the first of Rogers' inner conditions. You, as a manager, cannot force your employees to be open to new experiences. You can, however, create an atmosphere conducive to their openness to new experiences.

The more variety of creative activities and exercises that a person becomes exposed to, the faster they will become receptive to new ideas and change. Job rotations, greater use of team or partnership work assignments, and continuous training in skills, best practices, and improved thinking techniques will be a part of the commitment required. Allowing individual choice and participation in a variety of creativity-fostering programs and activities provides the greatest opportunity for inclusion and facilitates acceptance.

Attempting to force individuals to change their thinking or actions can be counterproductive and will not accelerate the desired result. Through enabling individual creativity in small increments, individuals will slowly expand their own comfort zones to become more open to change and innovation.

As individuals and organizations become more open to new ideas and experiences, they become more tolerant and flexible in their thinking. Change, growth, and experimentation through trial-and-error become part of the new culture. As the people who create the product, deliver the service, or deal with the customer become more fully functioning, they see more possibilities, seize more opportunities, and improve processes before problems arise.

Openness enhances opportunity-seeing and problem-solving. In a fully functioning structure, when a problem occurs with a service, the delivery person does not have to seek out a manager to make a decision. They make decisions on the spot. What were once fixed rules now become guidelines that open up possibilities, rather than restrict movement. This type of fluidity creates a process that encourages the individual to interact with situations, rather than react to them. It enables powerful possibilities rather than managed results and generates a better quality experience for everyone involved.

Managers who practice this open, receptive style will discover that employees will report a deeper sense of satisfaction and joy with their work and their lives.

Inviting the whole person to participate in the organization provides profound qualitative and quantitative changes for both the organization as well as the experience of the participant.

Internal Locus of Evaluation

An internal locus of evaluation can be generated only by the individual; however, a manager can encourage this development through providing a non-threatening, non-judgmental environment.

Companies and organizations with enlightened missions and confident leadership encourage decision-making at the lowest level. People who have been well-trained and clearly understand the objectives and mission of their organizations are capable of thinking and acting on their own. Individuals begin to trust their own internal direction, rather than deferring decisions or acting out of rote. Full functionality creates a sense of calm satisfaction as confidence and intelligence develops. This replaces the fear of making a wrong choice that too often disables or slows the process. Cross-trained individuals are comfortable thinking for themselves, are not in conflict with the group, and can act independently yet with regard for the group.

The Ability to Toy With Elements or Concepts

All work and no play limits an organization. Implementing constructive creativity is often encouraged through the process of mentally playing with a variety of seemingly unrelated elements and concepts. The playfulness, mental flexibility, and spontaneity we had as children defines the concept of innovation and creativity.

Managers must encourage synthesized thinking through play. Employees who look beyond their job descriptions and bring in ideas from other areas of their lives are most likely to see relationships between broad concepts. They observe what makes situations alike and think in fuzzy pictures, instead of sharp images. Skills acquired through unrelated previous employment, a hobby, or any other part of life can be utilized in the workplace. Synthesizers do not put borders around activities, do not place feelings and attitudes in individual boxes, and do not restrict their learning with structural impediments. Most inventions, improvements, and new ideas come out of this synthesized thinking.

The benefits of learning and valuing natural playfulness are demonstrated through increased hunches and more frequent insights. Intuitive powers are awakened. Ideation is more prolific. From these innovative processes and exercises are born tools that can transform the worker bee of the old paradigm into the innovative business partner of the fully functioning organization.

Psychological Safety

As people begin to exercise creative choices, they will encounter situations that can be fearful. Often they are making decisions they have never made before, trying things they have never tried before. Trusting intuition and moving ahead without logic or validation can be a scary process.

One of the basic tenets of creativity is that it can flourish only when the individual feels safe. If a manager is to encourage employees to exercise their full potential for the good of the organization, the manager must secure that safety and freedom for the employees. Typically, that means the manager must make it rewarding to be creative—to break from the norm while keeping the good of the organization in mind. Rewards must be focused on right efforts, not simply right outcomes. Slowly, as individual and collective creativity are fostered and valued, people will be encouraged to participate more and more.

Psychological Freedom

Empowerment is a common "buzz" word in business today. Power means to enable or be able to act. Literally, we might say it means to know what to do and doing it. Empowering employees is little more than providing the psychological freedom necessary to act.

Empowered self-learners become empowered self-leaders. At the Saturn automobile assembly plant, any individual can shut down the assembly line at any time for any reason. Each individual is empowered to make the decision for himself or herself. It does not require a committee, a consensus, or any outside approval.

The Price of Change

There will be resistance. When you begin to exercise more creativity in the workplace, you will be changing, and change does not come without discomfort. Old habits die hard; however, new habits take time to develop. Changing means dying to the old. Homeostasis, the tendency to resist change, fights against our efforts even when they are in our best long-term interests. Just as individuals resist exercise or healthy eating, knowing it is good for them, so will organizations resist change. Initially, change may feel like loss.

All gain of value is proceeded by loss—loss of control, loss of comfort, loss of confidence, and loss of habits. Persistence, however, is its own reward. The manager and the individual must be patient, understanding that this process must work itself through before a higher level of performance can be found. Short-term gains may need to be forfeited to ensure long-term gain, a concept that may meet with great resistance within some organizations.

Epilogue

"If everyone performed the same as me
what kind of world would this be?"
—Emil Crassner

How many times in your life have you felt that you had it all together: the moment when job, family, social life, spiritual life, everything seemed to be flowing along perfectly? Then . . . bang, everything seemed to fall apart. Something happened that challenged your thinking and the perfect moment was lost because you lost your perfect attitude. My friend Doug Bottorff writes, "There are no perfect conditions, only perfect people." Perfect people, he goes on to say, are people who are committed to growth and change.

Recently, I found myself in the line at the service desk at a large department store. Standing there, I listened to people as each returned or exchanged merchandise. Most of these people were angry. They complained. They were argumentative. They didn't seem to be having any fun at all. It occurred to me that they not only had the condition of having purchased a product that didn't work or fit, but they'd also decided to choose this event as a place to focus their feelings and consciousness. They hadn't chosen the condition, but they were choosing their attitude. They had allowed an event to degrade their attitude. It was a matter of where they chose to put their attention.

Attention is all you have to give in life. Focusing on the negative aspects of a situation creates negative feelings. Focusing on the positive creates positive feelings. It is so easy to understand this simple principle—but try explaining it to someone who is standing in the complaint line.

Sometimes we have imperfect conditions, such as an item that fails to deliver our expectations. Imperfect conditions are going to happen in life. Not everything works the way you want it to. Life isn't perfect.

Imperfect conditions challenge us daily. I once opened a can of corn only to find peas inside. We all had a good laugh and then decided that maybe someone felt we needed peas more than corn for dinner. Since some of the family still wanted corn, we also opened a second can of corn. We had corn and peas that night. Imperfect situation. Perfect outcome. The difference was our attitude—choosing the focus, and not letting emotions take us in an unproductive direction.

Fully functioning people realize that events or conditions aren't perfect. They understand that they are impersonal. They understand that where they put their focus determines their attitude in an event. They practice choosing their focus. Sometimes they do it better than others. It's a process. Through this process they learn to transform events from stressful to rewarding, and empower themselves through attitude regardless of events. People who have lots of crises have more opportunities to learn. People who encounter lots of hateful and negative people have lots of teachers. If you can't change the condition, change your mind. If you need practice, get a job at the service desk at a department store.

The young woman at the service desk understood these principles. To those unhappy customers, at that moment, this woman held the power of the organization in her hands. She understood that she did not have control of the event—however, she did have the authority to try for a win-win outcome. She understood that those complaints were not directed at her. Those were simply conditions.

Helping diffuse tense situations by staying relaxed, speaking calmly, exceeding the customers' requests, always being polite, and so on were processes she'd learned over time. None of those actions might make the customers' anger any less or their negativity any more positive, but that is not this woman's job. She is responsible for herself. Being responsible only for yourself is being a fully functioning person. Being her best may have a positive influence on someone who has had a bad day, or is experiencing a life crisis.

Nothing has a more profound impact on the quality of your life than the quality of your thinking. Cross-training points the way toward improving the quality of your thinking through seeing greater purpose in everything we do. It is the little choices that transform us. Each one makes a difference in every moment of our lives. We all have an impact on our self and others in everything we do. The informational energy we transmit ripples outward, touching many other lives. Even in your smallest actions, you are always growing or reducing the quality of your experience and the experience of those around you.

The minute your creative mind begins thinking in this fully-functioning way there is no turning back. As you begin seeing things from your expanded perspective, you move toward greater fulfillment, opportunity, and self-expression and and away from discomfort, unhappiness, and fear. You begin to bring your whole being into everything you do, every moment you are doing it.

Keep your creativity stimulated with additional reading.

A Whack on the Side of the Head and A Kick in the Seat of the Pants by Roger vonOech

Higher Creativity by Willis Harman and Howard Rheingold

Creative Visualization by Shakti Gawain

101 Creative Problem Solving Techniques by James Higgins

Using Both Sides of Your Brain by Tony Buzan

Writing the Natural Way by Gabrellia Ricco

Writing down the Bones and Wild Mind by Natalie Goldberg

This Is It or anything else by Alan Watts

Handbook to Higher Consciousness by Ken Keyes

The Mechanism of Mind, Serious Creativity, and *I'm Right and You're Wrong* by Edward DeBono.

The Future of the Body by Michael Murphy

On Becoming a Person by Carl Rogers

Creativity by Mihaly Csikszentmihalyi

Thinkertoys by Michael Michalko

You're Smarter Than You Think by Linda Perigo Moore

Waking Up by Charles Tart

99% Inspiration by Brian Mattimore

The Courage to Create by Rollo May

The Oxford Companion to the Mind
   by Richard Gregory, Editor

The Owner's Manual for the Brain by Pierce J. Howard, Ph.D

Idea Power by Arthur VanGundy

Evolution of Consciousness by Robert Ornstein

Creative Action in Organization by Cameron M. Ford
   and Dennis A. Gioia, Editors

Index